PRAYER: A NEW ENCOUNTER

PRAYER
A NEW ENCOUNTER

by

MARTIN THORNTON

MOWBRAYS

LONDON & OXFORD

2483
T n P

To

MONICA
My Wife in
The Trinity

Contents

Foreword

PRAYER, WORSHIP, spirituality — these constitute a major problem for the Church today. For many people, the traditional forms seem to have gone dead. Yet a purely secular or religionless Christianity has proved itself to be sterile, and there is plenty of evidence among the younger generation of a search for a viable spirituality.

Can the Church respond to this search? In the present book, Dr. Thornton shows us what such a response might be — a response that is intellectually honest and that takes both contemporary theology and the contemporary world seriously. I am especially pleased that Dr. Thornton has drawn so much on my own theological work in the writing of his book. His profound knowledge of ascetical theology has enabled him to draw implications from my work of which I was not myself aware, though for the most part I think these are consonant with my intentions.

While this book breaks new ground in spirituality, Dr. Thornton is well aware of the continuing value of the tradition, provided that we penetrate behind the conventional stereotypes to the living realities. "Any genuinely new spirituality," he writes, "will contain ancient elements within it, but reinterpreted and reformed." I believe that his book will make a major contribution to one of the great needs of our time.

JOHN MACQUARRIE

Personal Preface

MODERN THEOLOGY is an ancient concept, since every age has to make its own reappraisal and practical application of the faith once delivered to the saints. Sometimes this development takes the form of a gentle unfolding of tradition; sometimes, as is the case today, it is a radical upheaval. The present generation of Christians must learn to live with chaos, more positively they must grasp and live their faith in a spirit of adventure and experiment. The honest conservative who decries current trends may be fulfilling a useful purpose; nostalgia for a more comfortable past is a defiance of providence.

Much attention is being given to theological restatement, to new pastoral method, fresh means of communication, and experiment with liturgical and devotional patterns. Yet we are only beginning to appreciate that this is leading to a new literary form. This new style of theological writing appears to have three main qualities derived not from fashion but from the heart of contemporary theology itself. The first is a sane empiricism, even a subjectivism, by which the writer is permitted, or claims, considerable freedom in drawing upon his personal faith and experience. A few decades ago a theological writer could only propound an original idea — if he was bold enough to admit to one — by propping it up with as many references as he could dig out of Christian history. His idea was only acceptable if he could prove that St. Augustine, or St. Bonaventure, or William Temple, or preferably all three, had once said something very like it. The criterion of value was "objective" scholarship and its aim was the exposition of "objective" truth. We now see that theology can only arise from the experience of personal faith within the community of faith and that if the old-time scholar pushes his objectivity far enough he becomes a religious philosopher not a theologian.[1] The contemporary theological target changes from propositional truth to that which explains, interprets and guides faith-experience. All this derives from prevailing "existentialism", and whether we claim or disclaim this ambiguous label its influence cannot be discounted. Writing of the father of this movement, Roger L. Shinn says: "In true existentialist manner he derides the practice of separating the writing from the writer."[2] "Objectivity" was no goal for Kierkegaard.

As so often happens this new movement, with its new style of writing, turns out to have close associations with something very old indeed. We have learned that the Bible itself is no objective record of events and sayings, no set of revealed propositions, no manual of morals and no biography of Jesus. It is an intensely personal interpretation of the experience of the biblical writers from within the community of faith. St. Augustine's *Confessions*, the poems of St. Francis, St. John of the Cross, and John Donne, the *Revelations* of Julian of Norwich — not to mention Margery Kempe — are all deeply personal works in existential idiom. The hard core of ascetic theology comes down to us in the classic forms of community *regulae*, personal instruction, letters of direction and spiritual autobiography. It is deeply personal.

Secondly, and an incentive to this new style of writing, is the expansion of lay participation in all aspects of Church life, including the theological. The lay-theologian is nothing new but a new public has arisen which demands serious practical theology in a readable and relevant form. This demand is not for simple, or "popular", or non-technical writing — though it can well dispense with the esoteric jargons of academic vogue — but rather for practical theology of the broad sweep for educated Christians instead of the detailed minutiae of specialised scholarship. The need is for faith speaking to faith, with its personal element; for theology growing out of reflective experience leading to a reinterpretation of experience.

1. John Macquarrie, *Principles of Christian Theology* (S.C.M. Press, 1966), pp. 1–4.

2. Roger L. Shinn, *The Existentialist Posture*, from *Restless Adventure: Essays on Contemporary Expressions of Existentialism* (Scribner's Sons, 1968), p. 49.

A third quality of the new writing is its emancipation from convention, from respectability. Alan Watts' important and much-quoted *Beyond Theology*[3] is a good example of this style, but I doubt if it would have been accepted by a reputable publisher thirty years ago. *The Art of Godmanship* would never have been permitted as a subtitle for a serious work of theology, yet recently no less than the Lady Margaret Professor at Oxford called a book *God Talk*.[4] Even after making the indisputable point that this is a fair translation of the word "theology", I can imagine a staid sub-editor wishing to replace it by the subtitle *An Enquiry into the Principles of Religious Language*. This new approach is neither gimmick nor fashionable sloppiness, for behind it lies a vital principle. The theological author is no longer a cipher expounding objective truth but a person trying to guide others in the interpretation of a shared faith; his aim is not to instruct but to stimulate and inspire. This involves a personal and pastoral relationship between writer and reader, which is better served not by the style of the pedagogue but of the conversationalist or letter-writer. The style has certain precedents: I Corinthians hardly qualifies for a PhD. The time may come when the latest study in eschatology — heavenmanship — starts after the manner of *The Autocrat of the Breakfast-Table*: "I was just going to say, when I was interrupted . . ."

Apart from its content and subject matter, this book is something of an expriment. I shall do my best to avoid two pitfalls which confront any writer: the slavish attempt to copy the style of another writer, and the self-conscious effort to create a "style" of one's own. It would be foolish indeed to ape Watts, let alone Oliver Wendell Holmes, but although this is to be a speculative commentary on the work of another I shall try to remain true to the three principles just considered. I can think of nothing quite so depressing as my spiritual autobiography, and I do not intend to write it, but I shall not be frightened of personal experience. I am writing from faith to faith, from my own faith to that of others, and although I should be the last to put too much value on

3. Hodder and Stoughton, 1964.
4. John Macquarrie (S.C.M. Press, 1967).

religious feeling I doubt if any faith could survive for long without some of it. I shall try to write directly to the faithful, to my blood brothers and sisters in Christ, and not to some objective idol floating about in the academic air. I shall try to avoid the sillier sort of jargon that can be such fun in the senior common room and meaningless anywhere else. On the other hand I shall not assume the twentieth-century laity to be in the theological kindergarten: those who are do not read books.

I shall relax. If the book takes on a conversational sort of style then I shall deem it a successful outcome. If I fail in these background objectives it might still be worthwhile to have stated the ideal, and to have insisted that it is an ideal for others to aim at not a defect to be avoided.

Having said all that I make no apology for introducing this present book with critical references to some of my former work: it is the simplest way to do it. I spent practically the whole of my last book[5] trying to explain what that ambiguous phrase "pastoral-theology" really means, and it has only just occurred to me that this new style of theological writing is the obvious and necessary vehicle for its expression. Conversely, more and more theology is moving from the academic towards the pastoral form, and it might be worthwhile to summarise my main conclusions as to what this means.

First, pastoral-theology is an approach rather than a subject. It is closely allied to prayer and religious experience and attempts to bring out the practical implications of any branch of divine learning. A study in patristics can be pastoral-theology and a book on preaching can be thoroughly academic.

Secondly, pastoral-theology is the complement, ally and interpreter of "academic" theology. Within the totality of the Church's mission the two are inter-related not in opposition, and even the most esoteric scholarship may be a fruitful seed-bed for pastoral-theology.

Thirdly, pastoral-theology is a discipline in its own right, with a method that differs from that of academic theology but which is just as reputable. Pastoral-theology is neither third-rate scholarship, nor the practical know-how that usually comes under the

5. *The Function of Theology* (Hodder and Stoughton, 1968).

heading of pastoralia. This gives rise to a fourth point which was not very clearly brought out in the earlier book: it is that the modern Christian, deepening his faith by reading, or the pastor guiding him, must make his own theological adaptation according to circumstances. Pastoral-theology is that which makes such adaptation as easy as possible, but it cannot be written like a modern cook-book: take exactly these ingredients, in exactly these quantities, mix and bake for thirty-three minutes in an oven at 385 degrees and success is assured. Any experienced cook knows the fallacy of this approach. In the long run the vagary of the old fashioned recipe is more satisfactory: take apples (or pears), sugar (or honey), in "sufficient quantity", add spices, herbs and flavourings "to taste", bake in a moderate oven until nicely brown. That makes proper allowance for circumstances, experience and personal adaptation, and is analogous to good pastoral-theology.

Back in 1959 I published a book called *Christian Proficiency*[6] which has turned out to be quite a good example of this type of pastoral-theology. The advent of the new style in theological writing has at least clarified my own mind as to what I have been trying to do for the past twenty years. That book was based firmly and blatantly on Dr. E. L. Mascall's *Christ, the Christian and the Church*,[7] a work which, although studded with pastoral insights, was not easily adaptable to the Christian life of prayer. This is no criticism of Mascall but rather an example of the proper correlation between scholarship and pastoral-theology.

But of recent years the comparative success of *Christian Proficiency* — it refuses to go completely and decently out-of-print — has become an embarrassment: if not out-of-print it is disastrously out-of-date. A lot of water has flowed under the bridge during the last twelve years, and under the spiritual-theological bridge it has become something of a torrent. I hope the present book will replace *Christian Proficiency*, for I am convinced that the only solid basis for the modern spirituality for which we so frantically search is solid and responsible modern theology. The present pastoral-theological experiment is based not

6. S.P.C.K., 1959.
7. Longmans, Green, 1946.

on *Christ, the Christian and the Church*, but equally firmly and blatantly on John Macquarrie's *Principles of Christian Theology*.[8] The former appeared in 1946, the latter in 1966, and to see the differences between these two works is roughly to understand my own change of approach. In *Christian Proficiency*, my initial query was: "this is the living tradition of Christian prayer, what is its doctrinal basis and how should we continue in it?" Dr. Macquarrie suggests a different question: "I live in this world and I believe in the Creed, what do I do next?" Those who are familiar with the works of these two scholars will see the point. But it is of crucial importance to understand that they differ only in their philosophical framework and approach, while remaining in concord about the fundamentals of Christian doctrine. The difference in approach, moreover, is inspired and demanded by a total situation which has changed radically in the last twenty years. It is pertinent that *Principles of Christian Theology* was the subject of a most laudatory review-article by Dr. Mascall.[9]

A further word of explanation is required as to my use of Dr. Macquarrie's work. *Principles of Christian Theology* is a large book, a *Summa* twice the length of *Christ, the Christian and the Church*, and it is divided into three parts. The first part expounds the new philosophical background against which we are to review Christian doctrine, and which should lead to new insights into prayer, and even to new methods if such are desired. Obviously this background must be understood before we can get anywhere, and its exposition and simplification present me with a difficult task. Dr. Macquarrie is one of the new-style writers as well as being a contemporary theologian, so the simplest and best solution to the problem would be to refer the reader to the most relevant portions of his book.[10] I hope that many will adopt this course, but to leave the matter there would be to evade the duty of true pastoral-theology. Dr. Macquarrie is both readable and exciting, but he is also a scholar in the best sense of that word, concerned with substantiating his thesis by scholarly methods. Pastoral-

8. S.C.M. Press, 1966.

9. *Church Quarterly Review*, July, 1967.

10. Chapters III, V, *see also* Dr. Macquarrie's concise *Martin Heidegger* (Lutterworth Press, 1968).

theology is concerned only with his relevant conclusions, of which it must try to make practical use. This may mean resorting to analogies, metaphors and descriptive symbols which, while not being erroneous, might not stand up to pedantic criticism. These possible dangers must be pointed out in context, but if such pastoral explication is forbidden then a good deal of traditional spirituality — the nuptial analogy for example — must be ruled out of court: and there would be few legitimate sermons next Sunday.

The second part of *Principles of Christian Theology* is a contemporary interpretation of basic doctrine upon which a new spirituality is to be built. This section is our main concern. Part three, subtitled *Applied Theology*, will be used sparingly, which may sound curious. It could be suggested that either I am neglecting the most fruitful field for my purpose or that this section renders any further application superfluous, or even impertinent. To the first point I would reply that this third section bristles with practical insights to which I have nothing to add, and that other portions of it could well form the basis of another book. Were I to attempt a second study of Dr. Macquarrie's work on this section — and the idea is inviting — it would replace not *Christian Proficiency* but my even earlier *Pastoral Theology: a Reorientation*.[11] This presents another reversal of values between the nineteen fifties and the nineteen seventies. The earlier book dealt with the pastoral-theology behind parochial organisation, with the shape of the parish as microcosm of the body of Christ. *Christian Proficiency* was something of a sequel dealing with the life and prayer of individuals within that organism. If there are two pastoral-theological books in Macquarrie's *Principles of Christian Theology* its approach demands that we start the other way round: only after having studied individual human existence is it possible to discuss the community of faith in which it is expressed.

As to the second point — that of impertinence — Dr. Macquarrie himself draws a clear distinction between *applied* and *practical* theology[12] and he constantly declines to explore these fields in detail. For example: "Here again we touch on the border

11. S.P.C.K., 1956.
12. *Principles of Christian Theology*, p. 36.

B

of a special discipline without seeking to invade it — the discipline of ascetical theology."[13] Coupled with an earlier remark that "applied theology will provide the theological principles from which these specialised studies will move into their particular fields",[14] I hope that this book will be regarded as the acceptance of an invitation rather than as an impertinent trespass. Under this policy part three of *Principles of Christian Theology* contains an invaluable but comparatively short chapter on prayer and worship,[15] and this again might reasonably be construed as an invitation to elaborate.

But this is breaking the rules of pastoral-theological writing that I have set myself. It is being unnecessarily respectable because instead of regarding me as impertinent Dr. Macquarrie has freely offered me his approval, help and encouragement. I have received help from others, being particularly grateful to the trustees of the John Bohlen Lectureship who honoured me with this appointment in 1970 and gave me the stimulus of a semester at the Philadelphia Divinity School. Professor John E. Skinner kindly read the draft manuscript, offering suggestions, encouragement and criticism, while conversations with other members of the faculty, and discussions with my classes, added further insights.

Having said all that it might be asked why I have resorted to such an old-fashioned and academic expedient as footnotes. In the first rough draft I tried to do without them and every page seemed to consist of the name of the scholar I am trying to interpret in pastoral-theological terms, together with the title of his book, all within a veritable forest of brackets. Since this is admittedly a speculation on the work of another, and since I hope at least one or two will take it seriously enough to refer to the original, old-fashioned footnotes of reference seem the most workable method. Perhaps it will underline the point that I am not interested in modernity for fashion's sake.

13. *Principles of Christian Theology*, p. 442.
14. *Principles of Christian Theology*, p. 36.
15. *Principles of Christian Theology*, pp. 431–43.

PART ONE

I Live in this World

ONE

Why Change Anyway?

THE PRESENT generation of Christians must learn to live with chaos: it is a providential vocation. Nevertheless I have deep sympathy with the conservatives who have been faithful to the old ways and who view the present upheaval with apprehension and distrust. Why change anyway? Why cannot the wretched theologians leave things alone? There are numerous answers to these questions which may be grouped under two main headings: tradition and culture.[1]

At first sight *tradition* looks a curious reason in favour of change, but this points to a common misunderstanding. Tradition moves as an ever-flowing stream and the best way to understand it is to assume that it begins with the present moment, looks towards the future and moves back into the past. It is not something which began in the remote past, and which gets continually repeated — that would be antiquarianism — but a living thing, and life itself implies change: tradition develops. The dress and ceremonial of the yeoman at the Tower of London is antiquarian; apart from the possible loss of a tourist attraction it would make little difference if the yeomen were replaced by plain-clothed police. A thousand years before the building of the Tower of London, Christians were celebrating the eucharist but this is not antiquarian, it is traditional because it comprehends past, present and future. Every celebration is a startlingly new thing, every celebration is both like and unlike every other. Perhaps we could say that the eucharistic vestments, like the Beefeaters' uniform, is a pleasant bit of antiquarianism, while the eucharist itself is of tradition? Tradition has two particular qualities which are important to this discussion.

1. *Principles of Christian Theology*, pp. 10–13.

First, if tradition is a flowing stream it does not move at a uniform speed, if it meanders through the water-meadows for most of the time, while we laze happily in the boat, it occasionally turns into a waterfall and we find ourselves at the bottom, spinning around in a surging whirlpool. That is where we are at the moment, and the obvious hint of the analogy is that we cannot sail back up again. We can only go on, out of the whirlpool into a new reach of comparative order, a new vista of spiritual progress. I still have sympathy with the conservative, who is now hoping that the next lot of water-meadows will soon come into sight and that they will bear some resemblance to those he remembers: if tradition means what I take it to mean there will be such resemblances, but there must be differences as well. I also have sympathy with the responsible radical but not for the irresponsible sort: he does not need it anyway because he is revelling in the whirlpool and does not want to get out.

The second quality of tradition is that it not only starts with the present moment but it embraces the past within it. I think it was Herbert Butterfield who said something to the effect that the one thing history never did was repeat itself: we cannot sail up the waterfall to the last lot of meadows. Nevertheless, tradition presents cycles of recurring themes and some of the great teachers of the past have a habit of becoming startlingly topical. Any genuinely new spirituality will contain ancient elements within it, but reinterpreted and reformed. To change the analogy, a con· temporary building may be composed of old materials, reprocessed and brought together in a new design. Pastoral-theology is concerned with the present and the immediate future. It must be prepared to be courageously radical, cutting away useless accretions and ruthlessly pruning unproductive, if well-beloved, customs and practices. Yet half the method and technique of pastoral-theology consists in looking into the past tradition and rediscovering just those ancient elements which fit into the contemporary scheme of things.

Why change anyway? The second main heading in answer to the question is *culture*. Here is another ambiguous word, but I take it to mean that moral, intellectual and social climate which subtly pervades every particular age and society. It is that ethos, with its ideals, outlook and aspiration, which, despite individual divergences, binds a people together. This cultural influence on spirituality is well illustrated by the history of recent times.

The Oxford Movement inspired a new interest in prayer and worship, and to meet it the pastoral Tractarians looked to the spirituality of the Counter Reformation; the school of St. Teresa, St. John of the Cross and especially St. Ignatius Loyola. Although it is questionable whether this school of prayer fits readily into the English or Anglican tradition, it was nevertheless not a bad choice. Its rigid discipline, its concern for detailed method, its love of the timetable and above all its stress on duty, made it attractive to the Victorian and Edwardian outlook. The two cultures met in that not uncommon association of toughness and sentimentality; if this period in English history fell for discipline and duty it also lapped up a sugary devotion. Religion, like Victorian family life, became regimented, pious and respectable — at least on the surface — and if moving the morning service from eleven to ten a.m. caused consternation, family tea at three forty-five instead of four p.m. would have constituted an equally shattering upheaval. Eventually all this wore thin and a decade ago I had a hunch that instead of "devotion" the idea of "proficiency" might appeal to an age nurtured on technology. Proficiency is a medieval term indigenous to scholastic spirituality, and my appeal was away from seventeenth-century Spain and back towards Benedictinism — the "older spirituality" with its roots in the monastic experiments of the sixth century. I have claimed that this system is more orthodox and more biblical since its foundation is the doctrine of the Trinity, set within the Church as the family of God, and expressed through the three-fold *regula*: the eucharist, the divine office and personal devotion. But *Christian Proficiency* is now out-of-date: why is this? Although this system has served the Church well for fifteen hundred years, and has been proved to work in practice, it has admitted theological weaknesses which will be examined throughout this study. Under the present heading of change through culture it is being undermined by modern mobility. The original *Rule* was designed for a stable group of monks: stability was elevated into a fourth counsel of perfection. The Cistercians, with their monk-peasants, modified things a little, and the English

Reformers went still further in adapting the underlying principles
to suit a seventeenth-century rural economy. The Book of
Common Prayer is the Benedictine Rule adapted to the stable
English village.[2] Claiming support from the Cistercians, the
Friars, the Jesuits, and lesser sources, I have suggested such
further modifications as reducing the divine office to its efficient
ascetical minimum and taking it out of the choir into the train and
the bus; private recitation is not incompatible with common-
prayer. Frankly I am attracted to the classical ideal — including
its stability — and I have leaned over backwards to make it a viable
basis for a contemporary spirituality. Having exhorted the faithful
to be courageously open to the future I must admit to a reluctance
to throw over such a gigantic chunk of past tradition. Yet can a
spiritual system move from Monte Cassino to modern Manchester
without being "adapted" out of all recognition? Will further
modification strain the thing to breaking point? And what will this
system look like when its theological bases — the Trinity, the
Church, life recollected in Christ — are subject to modern reinterpretation? These are some of the questions with which we
shall be concerned.

But if Counter-Reformation ideals suited Victorian culture,
and if Benedictinism made sense up to 1960, where do we go now?
Has the tradition any hint of an age which fits more nearly with
modern culture? If it has it looks as if we must go back further still,
to the primitive era. For characteristic of the spirituality of the
New Testament and of the Church's first centuries was an unin-
hibited spontaneity; in spite of poverty and persecution there was
a childlike joy, even a gaiety about it. Not duty but cheerfulness is
the recurrent theme of early treatises on prayer. There was no
need to work at it grimly and painfully, no need for stereotyped
methods and techniques, no need to search for God for his prevenient presence was the plainest of facts. There was no need even
to go to church for there were no churches to go to. This is the
ideal to which modern Christians are attracted; it is later developments with their seemingly artificial disciplines, rules and duties
against which they rebel. Like their early brethren they have no
use for pious exercises, timetables and the rest, they want to know

2. See my English Spirituality (S.P.C.K., 1963), pp. 257–81.

God in simplicity, to see Christ in the world, to taste of the Spirit in everyday situations and in practical service.

To the Church in general and the Anglican tradition in particular, a return to the primitive has always been a worthy ideal; time and again this policy has saved the Church from exaggeration and error, it has cut through tangled accumulations of sophistry and brought cheerful gusts of fresh air into Christian living. The modern aim is estimable, but it poses a dilemma. The prayer of spontaneous simplicity is part and parcel of what Tillich and others have called the pre-theological age, when creeds, dogmas and formulae were undefined, and when speculation about the faith was vague, fluid, and not especially important. Conservatives may wish even more to return to so blissful a time but the present is not pre-theological, it is comparatively sophisticated and intensely interested in theology, possibly more so than any other age. We are a sophisticated society seeking for simplicity; a theological age that almost idolises experience.

A way out of the dilemma can be found in modern theology, for if not simple in itself it is a theology of simplicity, of integration. It begins, like the primitive period, with experience, and experience reflected upon produces theology, which in turn interprets and guides experience. This is the fundamental process: experience-theology-prayer.

Experience appeared first on our list,[3] not because it is to dominate the other factors as it has done in so-called "empirical" theologies, but because theology implies participation in a religious faith, so that some experience of the life of faith precedes theology and may indeed be said to motivate it. In this area of experience, as in every other, we seek to "make sense" of our experience, and the process of bringing the content of the faith-experience to clear expression in words embarks us on the business of theology.[4]

But with the passing of the primitive pre-theological age our Christian experience is usually second-hand. Religion begins with

3. of formative factors in theology.
4. *Principles of Christian Theology*, p. 5.

revelation, which Macquarrie divides into two types; "primordial" and "repetitive".[5] The incarnation is the Christian's primordial revelation which comes down to us through tradition: the Church, the Bible, sacraments, prayer and theology. By and large, modern people do not find their faith after the manner of St. Bernadette Soubirous: they do not return from a country walk having directly confronted a lady called Mary or a man whose name was Jesus. They do not even assume, after some more normal experience, that they have been aware of the divine presence — even if they have. Our faith depends on repetitive revelation which is enshrined in the creeds and, however attractive, we cannot return to the direct experience of the pre-theological age. Even if a modern agnostic was visited with something like the Damascus Road experience he would still need the Church and its doctrinal tradition to interpret it. There have always been, and we hope in God that there always will be, "unlettered" saints endowed with the gift of intuitive, contemplative vision of truth untrammelled by a lot of theology, those who will never be, and never need be, theologically articulate. But these favoured ones are still dependent upon the Church's tradition, and indirectly upon its theology.

Nevertheless we shall stick to the initial question posed by Macquarrie's approach: I live in this world, I believe in the creed, what do I do next? This leads to two further cultural implications which will be of importance to our study. Both are important in their own right, but they are especially pertinent here because they are both characteristic of the two ages with which we are concerned: the primitive pre-theological period and the present.

The first is that general philosophical outlook which we have come to know as existentialism. With this we shall be concerned throughout the book although it should not be necessary to enter too deeply into its technical ramifications. Suffice it to say that it forms part of both first and twentieth-century culture and that its influence cannot be withstood, whether or not particular men and women are interested in its technicalities. It is in fact only the professional philosopher or theologian, of conservative persuasion, who will oppose existentialism in learned books and lectures. But

5. *Principles of Christian Theology*, pp. 90–3.

neither they, still less the man-in-the-street, can escape from it as part and parcel of current culture. For it is at heart that approach to life which begins with experience and moves out into responsible activity, which is interested not so much in what things are but in how they act. Even modern science is existential because it moves beyond the pure observation and classification of phenomena to the practical uses to which its discoveries can be put. Ethics, Christian or otherwise, are now existential because they place the emphasis on free and responsible decision rather than on given legal codes. Most of contemporary theology is existential — whether we like it or not — because it is concerned not so much with proofs for God's existence, neither with his static, objective attributes, but with how he acts. No one is interested any more in how, still less when, God created the universe, but in his active concern for it, with his practical action within it. If this outlook is characteristic of modern life it is equally so of the primitive age of Christianity, with its overwhelming sense of God's activity in history, of the presence of the resurrected and glorified Christ, and of the inspiration of the indwelling Spirit ruling life and superseding laws, codes and systems. The spontaneous, contemplative prayer of this age was in fact trinitarian, Christological and redemptive, but it was centuries before these doctrines were formulated, and before the moralists and casuists started to reformulate laws and rules in Christian terms. When this theology did emerge it was couched in terms of prevalent Greek thought of a metaphysical, substantive, static kind, and it is this philosophical background which needs to be changed if current existentialism is to link up with that of the early centuries.

The second characteristic of both ages, or rather the characteristic of the first age to which we aspire today, is inherent in the existentialist approach. If the emphasis is not on God's remote existence and substantive attributes but on his activity then, following traditional theology, this activity must be a continuous ongoing process. So prayer, in its deepest essence, becomes a *continuous relationship* between man and God, whether or not that relationship is recognised or articulated. It is this faith-relationship which gave primitive prayer its spontaneity, simplicity and joy, and it is the ideal sought after in modern life, manifested in

popular notions like God in the midst, not on the pious perimeter
of life, or of Christ seen in others not only in sacrament and taber-
nacle. Prayer is no isolated devotional exercise but living relationship, it is not something one does but, primarily, something that is.

The classical vocabulary of prayer makes the relevant distinction between "act" and "habit". Habitual prayer — St. Paul's
"pray without ceasing" or the "'practice of the presence of
God" — has ever been the Christian ideal, and it has been
achieved by the tradition of disciplined acts, or particular occasions of prayer, embodied in the Benedictine *regula* of the eucharist, the divine office and specific acts of personal devotion.
There is absolutely no doubt that this system has proved itself over
and over again: it works. Nevertheless this time-honoured system
has always been subject to criticism, and its shortcomings will crop
up from time to time throughout our study. Suffice it to say that
the idea of a series of acts — prayers, meditations, offices and sacraments — leading into an habitual recognition of the divine presence, at least gives the impression that we somehow achieve, by
our own efforts, a continuous relationship with God. However
firmly we insist on prayer as response to prevenient grace, on the
divine initiative in all prayer-relation, this emphasis on rules,
duties, timetables and the rest is bound to risk an unhealthy subjectivism. The post-Benedictine spiritualities think in terms of forg-
ing a relation with God, the earlier ages joyously accepted this
relation as a fact of faith. We cannot return to the pre-theological
age, although its ideals are plainly those which we seek. The way
out is in reframing basic theism in contemporary terms.

If prayer in its primary sense is this living, continuous relation
between man and God, then prayer in its secondary and more
usual sense of specific acts of devotion, offices, sacraments and so
on, is its focus, or concentrate, or articulation. Macquarrie frequently employs this idea of concentration, or intensification of a
total existence (of which word much more later) with reference to
worship and the sacraments. Jesus is spoken of as focus or
"symbol" of the divine omnipresence, his eucharistic manifestation being a concentrate of the redeemed universe: ideas
which are traceable to the School of St. Victor, if not to Irenaeus.

All this is in line with tradition, but a rediscovered and re-interpreted tradition. Once we reverse the Benedictine order and see habitual relationship with God as primary prayer, and acts — saying prayers — as secondary, then we are back to the values of the primitive age, and we have simplified things enormously. If prayer is relationship with God and acts of prayer — or periods of prayer or just prayers — are foci or concentrates of it, then it is obvious that prayer and life are the same thing. If an act of prayer, in church, or in private, or even a long period of solitary silence, is an articulated concentrate of faith-experience, then it cannot be misinterpreted as withdrawal, or escape, from life. If we started the other way round, with St. Benedict, it would be possible to explain how the prayers and offices of the *regula* lead into habitual prayer and generally impinge on everyday living, but it does take a bit of explaining. There is far less need, or no need at all, to explain the relation between a field of vanilla-beans and concentrated essence of vanilla: the reference is patently to the same basic stuff.

If further explanation of this point is required it may be found in one of the most ancient of all analogical traditions in the history of spirituality: in the nuptial analogy with its roots in the Song of Songs and recurring in every age. Prayer is a marriage-relation with God, not a flirtation carried on by a series of clandestine meetings; it is a perpetual state and a continuous relation, varying in intensity and concentrated in acts: the sexual — and eucharistic – union, the embrace and the intimate conversation. And the relation may sometimes be enhanced and enriched by occasional separation. The analogy need not be laboured. The practical issue is for modern Christians to put things this way round, to see prayer as relation forged by sacramental bonds and involving total faith-commitment. Once this is established the acts look after themselves; they can be enjoyed without fuss or tension, with cheerfulness.

But if experience is prior to its interpretation, or if prayer is prior to theology, theology is necessary as guide and interpreter of prayer-experience. Theology embraces particular cultures and a return to pre-theological simplicity demands a new interpretation of the primordial revelation. Our premise remains — I live in this world and I believe in the creed — but this now raises a question which confuses and worries many of the faithful. What does it mean to express faith in the creed and yet want to reinterpret it? What is wrong with the creed as it stands? How will its reinterpretation help? If all this theologising is necessary how can we honestly say that we believe in the historic creed as it now stands in the Prayer Book? Is this creed — the one we solemnly recite in public worship — true or not? Or do we say it with tongue-in-cheek reservations? My straight answer to this is that I believe in the creed, wholly, completely, if you like dogmatically. I am willing to swear with all the intellectual integrity I can muster that it is true, and I shall not depart from this position. Nevertheless we have fallen into the old trap of asking the substantial, or academic, question rather than the existential one: the creed is true but how does it work? Theology is a tool not an idol, as guide and interpreter of experience it is subservient to prayer: "a theology that becomes an end in itself can easily degenerate into a rarefied academic speculation that has lost sight of the existential realities out of which it arose".[6] On the same point Macquarrie quotes Karl Rahner: "the clearest formulations, the most sanctified formulas, the classic condensations of the centuries-long work of the Church in prayer, reflection and struggle concerning God's mysteries; all these derive their life from the fact that they are not end but beginning, not goals but means, truths which open the way to ever greater truth".[7] So the creed is to be used, not merely understood, still less subserviently assented to.

How do we use the creed? If it is a tool not an idol a modicum of expertise is involved, and our acceptance of Macquarrie's reinterpretation further suggests that, without wavering in our loyalty to its truth, the tool might need a little sharpening and repair — perhaps a thorough overhaul — before it recovers its pristine efficiency. How is the creed "true"?

6. *Principles of Christian Theology*, p. 34.
7. *Principles of Christian Theology*, p. 165, re *Theological Investigations*, Vol. 1, p. 149.

TWO

Old Maps

WE HAVE come up against the problem of religious language[1] which no modern study can avoid. All language is in some sense technical in so far as its meaning varies according to context: "bowling a maiden over" means getting a girl to fall for you or performing a certain feat on the cricket field, depending on the circumstances in which the phrase is used. "Language cannot properly be understood in abstraction from the concrete living situation where it is *in use*, in this case, from the existential context of the community of faith."[2] This supports what has been said in the Preface; that religious language is personal, speaking from faith to faith, but this does not reduce it to mere opinion or prejudice.[3] This is obviously true of the creed which does not begin with a substantive statement like "God exists" but with the personal, existential, "I believe . . .", and it is followed by a series of clauses in different types of technical language: symbolism, history, analogy and myth. Most Christians recognise this and permit the ancient phrases to make their impact of faith without bothering too much about precise theological definition. This is legitimate, especially in the liturgy, but it is not putting the creed to its fullest use: as the basis of a total prayer-relation and as a guide life. For this the creed must be studied, meditated upon, expounded and reinterpreted, and I hope to show that this perennial process, far from being an unfortunate necessity, is itself a stimulating guide and interpreter of religious experience. So we return to the prior question: *how* is the creed true?

An enlightening attempt to explain the problem of religious

1. *Principles of Christian Theology*, pp. 111–33.
2. *Principles of Christian Theology*, p. 404.
3. *Principles of Christian Theology*, p. 114–15.

statement is contained in the analogy of the map, an idea employed by many linguistic theologians but perhaps more especially associated with the thought of I. T. Ramsey. A creed is a map of revealed truth, and it is "true" in exactly the same way as a map is "true". This analogy will repay closer examination because, in spite of its popularity, I do not think that its practical and pastoral implications have been fully brought out.

The relation between a map and the country it surveys is analogous to the relation between a creed and the reality it describes. The map is not the country any more than the doctrine of the Trinity is God, but properly used they are both accurate guides: the map will lead you through the country and the creed will inspire and interpret prayer in the light of revelation. If the map is not the country it depicts then neither is it the journey through that country, and it is the process of travelling that normally constitutes the map's usefulness. This illuminates Karl Rahner's remark that a classical formula is not an end but a beginning: you study the map before setting out on a journey, and there is little point in studying it if you do not intend to go anywhere.

It is indeed possible for a professional cartographer to derive intellectual satisfaction from the study of maps, yet their prime purpose is as navigational guides; they are not primarily produced to be understood, or believed in, still less argued about for amusement. The theologian, similarly, may become absorbed in theology for its own sake; St. Bonaventure described it as beautiful, as aesthetically satisfying like numbers to a mathematician or geometry to an architect. This is good and important, beauty and utility go together. Maps, too, may be very beautiful things, especially old ones which people frame and hang on their walls, but that is not their primary, existential purpose: it is not what they are *for*.

I am not upholding the pragmatic view of theology which teaches that dogmatic statements have *only* a practical value. I am not saying that the creed is only true if it somehow or other works out in practice, but rather that it works out in practice — as interpreter of experience and guide to prayer — because it is true in the first place. It is true in any case, whether we use it or just look at it, but putting it to its navigational function demonstrates its truth.[4]

There are different kinds of maps, all reliable yet none is exhaustive in the information it gives: no amount of theology will adequately describe God. Sometimes these different kinds of map are best used in combination; a simple road map will take us from one town to another, but we need a street-map when we get there, and perhaps a third map to point out buildings of special interest. We shall see that the old credal map is in many ways unsatisfactory as a modern guide, yet it brings out truths which the new map is apt to overlook: we shall need them both, the one illuminating the other. This analogy becomes more enlightening as we examine some of the different types of map, and it will offer suggestions to which reference can be made later.

First, maps like creeds vary in *date*: without being wrong they can both become obsolete. I have a map of Dorset produced by Robert Morden in 1740. It is an accurate map of identical outline and structure as the most recent Ordnance Survey. The place-names are sometimes spelt differently but they are recognisable and correctly sited. It marks no roads but it does tell me that the village in which I live is situated in Eggerdon Hundred. That is a truth which cannot be denied and it is of historical interest, but from a practical point of view there could hardly be a more useless piece of information: the Lord of the Manor is unlikely to want to enlist me in the local militia. It would be far more useful to know that this village came under the jurisdiction of Bridport Rural District Council. Perhaps Eggerdon Hundred is analogous to the clause in the creed that states how Christ "suffered under Pontius Pilate". It is important to know that Our Lord's Passion was a truly historic event, that it really happened in a certain place at a particular time. That is why this clause found its way into the creed, and I am convinced of its truth, but the name of the local governor has no relevance to my present experience of Christ.

My Dorset map has little green pictures of woods and marshes, and hills appear as little yellow humps of various shapes and sizes. These are strictly to scale, accurate in extent and elevation, and in

4. *Principles of Christian Theology*, p. 115.

C

exactly the right places. The map is true, yet a more up-to-date presentation of the same facts would be more serviceable. Nevertheless, if I wanted to walk from Bridport to Dorchester this old map would not let me down; properly read it would get me there, even without any roads. The Apostles' creed is not unlike my Dorset map. It will never let you down, it is true, but it must be properly read and in terms of living prayer and experience this is sometimes very difficult. If it is not pushing the analogy too far it looks as if this old map — true as it is — requires one or two supplementary aids before we can use it with confidence. A compass would be a help, or perhaps directions from village to village could be sought from passers-by? The creed needs this interpretative apparatus: a little Greek perhaps? Or some knowledge of biblical typology? That "He ascended into heaven, And sitteth on the right hand of God the Father Almighty" is suggestive of a little yellow hump in the middle of Eggerdon Hundred: it is true enough, I believe it with all my heart, but is this the only way, or the most illuminating way, of describing my living experience of God the Holy Trinity? Is this the most practical guide to prayer as a trinitarian interpretation of life? Perhaps, after all, a more modern road-map would get me from Bridport to Dorchester more easily, and indeed more safely. And this is the point: our quest is to make things easier not more difficult, to simplify not to complicate. Admitting that contemporary reinterpretation of doctrine takes some getting used to, our purpose is to make Christian life simpler and more meaningful to ordinary people. We shall be moving towards a more modern map, from Robert Morden to John Macquarrie, not to be fashionable, or for reasons of apologetic, still less for a little sophisticated theological fun, but because it makes prayer more relevant, spontaneous and exciting: in fact more primitive, and more cheerful.

Secondly, maps vary in *scale*. A map of the British Isles on a quarto sheet — about one hundred miles to an inch — cannot provide much detail. Comparatively windy roads look straight, lanes and villages do not appear at all. This map is also true, it is not wrong, it is simply not large enough to give more than a basic outline. Again the creed is a map on this kind of scale, it contains the fundamental direction of Christian revelation, it sets the primary course and gives the essential keys to Christian experience, it marks the life of prayer in outline. If we take the spiritual journey seriously, if we seek a map to use, not just assent to, we shall come to the point when other maps, on a larger scale, will be needed. A popular and primitive ideal is to meet with Christ not only in the sanctuary but in society, in other people. The Apostles' creed tells us that Jesus Christ is the Son of God and the son of Mary: God and man. The Nicene creed and the *Quicunque Vult* elaborate a little; they are maps on a slightly larger scale. But they do not explain how we can initiate a relationship with Christ, God, man and Henry Smith all mixed up together. Does this doctrine make any sense of Christian experience? If Christ is in the market-place, or in Henry Smith, how do you go about meeting him? Or is all this just devotional sentiment? To answer these questions we shall have to look at another map on a larger scale, a specifically christological map, and then we shall have to update it.

I am not departing from my premise — I live in this world and I believe in the creed — neither am I discarding the ideal of an efficient minimum of theology as a practical guide to life. The creed is a beginning not an end, a small-scale outline map, and we shall not resort to larger scale maps unless or until experience makes them necessary. The redrawing of the old credal map in more contemporary terms — the movement from Morden to Macquarrie — should reduce rather than increase the amount of theology needed by ordinary Christians who take their faith seriously. This policy will protect us from getting lost amongst the intricacies of maps drawn on an enormous scale. I have one of the village which covers most of the drawing-room floor — twenty-five inches to the mile — and which marks every house, footpath, pond and coppice, naming every farm and giving the acreage of each field. It is interesting and useful to those few hundred of us who live in the village, but if you wanted to go from Exeter to Edinburgh it would not be much help. Need I add that some of the doctoral theses from the universities are of this kind? Three hundred pages of commentary on the Epistle to Philemon might constitute worthy research from which a pastoral-theologian could deduce practical value, but it is not the sort of map to take on a long journey.

This brings us to the third main heading. There are *specialist* maps, relevant to the lives of ordinary people but misleading if used for the wrong purpose. Most school atlases begin with several pages of maps of the British Isles, all of the same outline but designed to depict special features: county boundaries, density of population, types of agriculture, geological sub-strata, average rainfall and so on. It would be a hopeless tangle if you tried to get all that information on a single sheet, and some of these maps can be very specialised indeed. I have an exciting one showing the distribution of archeological sites in Wessex, so we should not be too hard on the scholarly tome on Philemon. The important thing is to recognise the specialist maps for what they are and use them, or forgo using them, accordingly.

The most glaring example of misuse is the biblical atlas. This is used as a quarry for proof-texts to support any sort of personal prejudice. The Sermon on the Mount is regarded as a simple exposition of Christian ethics. The Book of Genesis has even been taken for a scientific treatise. All of which is like searching for an archeological site on Dartmoor armed with a map that is concerned with average annual rainfall in Scotland. There is nothing wrong with any of these maps, certainly not with the biblical atlas, or even with Philemon at twenty-five inches to the mile, but they must be used for the purposes for which they were designed.

Specialist maps of a particular country are drawn within the same general outline, and they may usefully be used in combination; you will need a road map to get within walking distance of the archeological site. In the next chapter we shall outline the new map, then gradually fill in the details, which should simplify our spiritual journey. But frequent reference will be made to the old one and the two will illuminate one another. The eucharistic rite, for example, is the same map in outline as the creed, and participation in that rite goes some way in expounding the creed and bringing it to life. The first part of the *Quicunque Vult* is the same outline map as the *Rule* of St. Benedict and, on a larger scale, as St. Augustine's *De Trinitate*. They all explore the country of trinitarian doctrine but in different ways and for different purposes. The second portion of the *Quicunque Vult* bears a similar relation to the Chalcedonian Definition and to St. Bernard's system of prayer: they are all christological, but they are drawn for different reasons. The St. Benedict–St. Bernard type of map formed the basis of *Christian Proficiency*, for these are traditional adaptations of the creed for the specialised purposes of spiritual theology. They still deserve the greatest respect and cannot be completely discarded, but we are attempting to by-pass them in our quest for primitive simplicity, returning to the creed itself. I live in this world and I believe in the creed implies that I want to redraw the map not only in a theoretical way but also from experience: I want to redraw it by getting out into the country with quadrant and theodolite.

Analogical speculations of this kind can be continued indefinitely and they easily become overstrained. It has to be admitted that there is a certain artificiality about our premise, for as we shall explain later[5] "I live in this world" is not quite so simple as it sounds. It embraces a life of prayer, study and doctrinal absorption which cannot be forgotten, and since any theology can be written only from within the community of faith it implies a continuing life of worship: it would be a little unrealistic for me to forgo Holy Communion until my experiential interpretation of the creed demanded it. Nevertheless the Counter-Reformation and Benedictine by-passes are realities on my map; quadrant and theodolite will play their part as well as pen and textbook: I live in this world *and* I believe the creed, but for the present I withhold dogmatic assent to any specific school of prayer, however venerable.

At the further risk of overstraining the analogy two small points remain. There are those who would jettison all the maps and rely on common sense, or intuition, or the "simple gospel", or even the inspiration of the Holy Spirit. This is like undertaking a long journey guided only by one's innate bump of direction. It might come off, but it is a precarious way to travel; a far too simple quest for the first-century ideal. Or the journey might be negotiated by reliance on signposts, traffic-signs and so on, but this is going to the opposite extreme because these are all based on the original map. They are systems like those of the Middle Ages and Counter-Reformation, and they can be more complex and confusing than

5. *See* Chapter 4 below.

the map itself. Nevertheless an occasional road-sign may be of assistance and this explains what I have just said about the eucharist: if a huge sign on a straight motorway says, London one hundred and sixty miles, it would be superfluous to re-examine the map every ten minutes.

The second small point leads into the next chapter. My Morden map of Dorset hangs on a wall, suitably framed. It depicts that delectable county in a delightfully picturesque and old-fashioned way. It almost asks to be looked at and admired, the wall is its proper place, a heavy glazed frame its proper setting. My road map is kept in the car, soiled and crumpled and that is *its* proper place; it suggests movement, use, journeying. It has no delightful little forest pictures or yellow humps for hills but roads running through modern contours, leading sometimes to ominous dark brown elevations that seem to challenge me to negotiate the peaks and ridges: it invites action. This is a meaningful analogy distinguishing the ancient creed from modern theology. The former is written in static terms, it speaks of bare facts and historic events, and it comes down to us in lovely cadences inviting liturgical song. But is it just a little too otherworldly, or even "olde worldie", to be of practical use? It would hardly be out of place illuminated, framed and hung on the wall, more often the church wall, for it would look comic anywhere else. The new map is more workmanlike, written in terms of action and movement, of experience and relationship.

I am no longer interested in how — let alone when — God created the universe, but rather with his active concern for it day by day. I have become tired of trying to define grace and classifying it into different types: I am asking how it works, what it is supposed to do to me. The ancient controversies about how Christ enters the consecrated elements on the altar are dead, but I do want to know how he acts through the eucharist and how I can best respond. All this points to practical help rather than bewildering hindrance from modern restatements of traditional doctrine. Now I must outline the new map.

THREE

The New Map in Outline

MACQUARRIE'S SYSTEM of philosophical theology, which forms the foundation of his exposition of Christian doctrine, is written in language which he calls — with apology for the clumsiness of the term — *existential-ontological*.[1] The two words in this fearsome phrase roughly correspond to the two parts of my premise. I live in this world, concerned with my total experience, is the existential starting point. I believe in the creed, which deals with a given revelation, introduces the ontological factor. Again very roughly, the first inclines towards the subjective and immanent, the second towards the objective and transcendent. If prayer is a continuing relation the existential approach deals with my side of it and the ontological with God's side. The very idea of prayer as relation gives an overwhelming importance to the hyphen.

This sounds very orthodox. What is so new about it, and how does this language differ from that of the old creed? Briefly to summarise the differences should help to clarify the practical significance of the new language. First, we are dealing with a single language-pattern whereas the creed is written in several different ones: symbolism, history, analogy, metaphor and myth. It would be a sophisticated exercise, though happily an unnecessary one, to sort out which particular clauses came under which heading. What sort of linguistic mode are we using when, for instance, we refer to God as "Father"? What is implied by calling Christ both "his only Son" and "our Lord"? Is "He ascended into heaven", or "And sitteth on the right hand of God", myth, metaphor or history? What does it mean in practice? The creed is true, and it is still an admirable exposition of faith for

1. *Principles of Christian Theology*, pp. 149–50, 167–70, 269–76, *passim*.

scholars trained in biblical, patristic and philosophical theology. It is the ordinary man who needs the new map.

Secondly, the old creed is heavily weighted on the abstract side. Despite its opening words it is composed of a series of descriptive truths of revelation. It is metaphysical in a way that the scholar may find intellectually satisfying; after a laborious study he might even find that it impinged on his practical life, but this is by no means obvious to the man-in-the-street. In fact the man-in-the-street is only asked to "believe" in it, that is to give either a sub-servient or intellectual assent. He is not invited to use it, or better to "have faith" in it, which must involve him in a commitment to the truth it enshrines. To make a classical distinction, "belief" is cognitive, "faith" is conative; the one means intellectual under-standing and assent, the other involves willing and striving.[2] A reinterpreted creed has to begin with "I have faith in . . ."

Thirdly, the old creed states a series of facts and truths which may ultimately guide practical life but the connection is far from plain. In three separate paragraphs it speaks of Father, Son and Holy Ghost but we have to move on to the *Quicunque Vult* before there is any clear idea of God as Trinity in unity which, we shall see, is the basis of practical life and prayer. In redrawing the map, therefore, I propose examining the fundamental doctrines of practical importance which are contained in it, rather than trans-lating it clause by clause. When I say that I believe in the creed I mean that I put my faith in those central doctrines common to the three historic formulae. When the new map emerges it will be based on the Apostles' creed, but will draw points which are more explicit in the Nicene creed and the *Quicunque*.[3]

We must now return to our new foundation lan-guage — *existential-ontological* — and try to grasp its signi-ficance. I advisedly use this pastoral-theological phrase instead of "understand the meaning". This itself is a relevant distinc-tion for to grasp the significance of something is very near to having faith in it, which invariably calls forth action; to under-stand the meaning is only an intellectual concept. The former

2. *See*, e.g. F. R. Tennant, *Philosophical Theology* (C.U.P. 1969), Vol. I, pp. 46, 297–305.
3. *See* p. 118 below.

phrase is certainly not irrational, but neither is it academic; it rather points to a total wisdom comprised of both reason and intuition which is so often the guide to practice in many spheres of life. If a farmer sees a field smothered in mayweed he grasps the significance that the soil is sour and needs liming; he does not have to be an agricultural scientist, chemically analysing his soil and understanding precisely why mayweed flourishes on acidity, or why and how chalk neutralises it. In a similar way most serious Christians grasp the significance of the eucharist without being able to give a coherent account of the theology involved.

Macquarrie himself hints at the validity of this pastoral-theological approach when he writes: "*Ontology* is the study of Being. Man is said to be *ontological* because, even if he never explicitly studies Being, he has to decide about his own being in the very act of existing."[4] Perhaps we could translate: "even if he never explicitly studies theology, he has to decide about his own faith in the very act of prayer." To grasp the insignificance is all-sufficient. And it is in this sense that most people, having never heard of Heidegger, Sartre, Kierkegaard, Jaspers, Bultmann and so on, are now existentialists: it is part of modern culture, an outlook subconsciously absorbed and grasped.

At the risk of certain pedantic traps, let us begin by defining "existence" as human experience in the actual, concrete world, with its activity and movement, its anxiety, choice, potentiality, development and death. What matters is not some theoretical essence or substance or soul, not some rule or convention, not some abstract or metaphysical philosophy, but simply me, now. If prayer is part of this experience, a continuous relationship between me and God, I still start with the existential *me*. Is not this attitude both impious and heretical? Is not the most axiomatic fact about any faith that of divine prevenience? Does not God always act first and then man makes his response? Yes, this is a valid objection — which will be overcome by the ontological side of our foundation — but it needs little reflection to see that to begin with my own experience is the realistic way of things. I am not suggesting that I am more important than God, but that I can have no valid experience of God until I have come to terms with, and

4. *Martin Heidegger*, p. 62.

become aware of, myself. In other words I am interested in the
living God of the Hebrews, not the theoretical God of the philosophers. I am concerned with the God who enters my experience,
not the Sunday School God I was told that I ought to believe in.
This is true of any theology, however transcendental it makes itself
out to be. A thinker like Karl Barth — or perhaps it would be
fairer to say early Karl Barth — can reject all natural religion, all
religious experience, he can renounce the integrity of human
reason and reduce prayer to the level of Pelagian works. He can so
stress the divine transcendence as to reduce our knowledge of God
to the biblical revelation and absolutely nothing else. But it is still
Barth who is making this point and it is Barth's subjective "me"
that is adopting this policy. In fact it is only Barth who can decide
that Barth is of no importance compared to God.

This is the reason for beginning — and only beginning — from
the existential standpoint. More serious is the charge of impiety,
and I must reject that significant strand of spiritual tradition
which regards the self — not selfishness or self-centredness but the
human self — as the diabolical enemy. "God is all and I am
nothing" sounds devout and humble, and no doubt it can be made
to bear a valid devotional meaning, but existential common-sense
must treat it as pious nonsense. It either means some sort of un-
Christian mystical absorption into God, or it is an insult to God
who created me. If you argue that I am an unworthy sinner, a
fallen and depraved creature, then I agree; but to say I am therefore nothing is a backhanded compliment to God who died on a
cross for my redemption.

If the existential approach begins with my experience, it means
total experience in the world. Such experience embraces the whole
being, not only the mind but passions, emotions, feeling and in-
stinct as well. Full, deep life — "authentic existence" — means the
integration of the complete personality, the wholeness or holiness
of human being. As a simple, non-technical synonym for "existence" I suggest "being-aliveness". This is in line with the Christian
tradition, which has its roots in the Old Testament; man is a
unity, not a composite of mind, body, spirit, and all the rest of the
psychological categories. But to see this old tradition in a new light
has important repercussions on spirituality.

It cannot be very happy, for example, with scholastic distinctions like sins of the "flesh" and of the "spirit"; with "mental" prayer and "affective" prayer, "vocal" prayer and prayer of silence. In practice these distinctions will remain but an existential approach to prayer will not make too much of them. The ancient nuptial analogy again helps: prayer is relationship, which expresses itself in acts of intercourse, conversation, silent companionship, practical service and so on, but all this is one, single, integrated life-relation, not to be carefully classified, regulated and scheduled. This approach would certainly be unhappy with the kind of discursive, three-point meditation associated with St. Ignatius Loyola: memory, imagination, intellection, volition, are not to be regarded as isolable parts of fragmented man, for human existence means total response. The point will recur throughout our study that ideas like integration, authenticity or harmony point to those forms of prayer to which Christian theology gives the generic if ambiguous name *contemplation*.[5]

Human existence — my existence — is always in-the-world. In one sense humanity is at-one with the rest of creation, he is part of it, while in another sense he stands out from it. Here is the classical dilemma about the "right use of creatures", but if it remains a dilemma our approach comes down heavily on the side of world-affirmation.[6] Existentialism in the way that, following Macquarrie, we use the term offers no justification for the exploitation of created things for selfish ends, or for self indulgence of any kind[7] but it speaks of our relation with the created universe in terms of love, redemption and harmony. Harmony with creation is again a form, in fact the initial form, of contemplative experience, which is to be nurtured not suppressed. This puts our approach in direct opposition to the later doctrine of "detachment from creatures", or to any form of Puritanism in the strict sense of a quest for pure spirit — "angelism" — with its distrust of the emotional and physical. We have already agreed not to make such fragmented psychological distinctions.

The third characteristic of our existential approach is that it

5. *See* Chapter 12 below.
6. *Principles of Christian Theology*, p. 238.
7. *Principles of Christian Theology*, pp. 239–42.

stresses not theory but action. Existentialism is not an academic philosophy but a practical outlook, a stance, a way of life. Its statements are invariably put in the form not of objective facts but of challenges, calls to action and decision. To say that there is a train from London to York at twelve twenty is a substantive statement, to which a normal reaction is — well what about it? The existentialist would say hurry up if you want to catch the twelve twenty to York. That is challenging, whatever the circumstances: if you intend to go to York it calls to action, you must hurry up. But even if you have no intention of going to York the statement still calls for a responsible and conscious decision; even if going to York never entered your head you must now consciously choose not to. If I believe means I assent to, the old creed follows with a list of substantive statements; there is a God who created the universe, to which a not unreasonable reaction would be: how interesting, I often wondered where it all came from, now who led the queen of spades, let's get on with the game. The existentialist would say Look out God is after you, which is a statement that cannot be shaken off so easily: it offers a challenge. You must either dismiss the challenge with a positive assertion of disbelief, or yield to God and allow him to catch you: you are forced to a decision.

Existentialism we have described not as a philosophy but as a way of life, and that is frequently said of Christianity itself. But in the latter case it too often implies a comfortable apathy rather than an honest rejection of abstract intellectualism. It degenerates into being a decent fellow and going to church, in adopting a vague and often negative morality. Existentialism on the other hand is a way of total commitment, engagement, responsibility and action. Its most practical key words are challenge, decision, and choice, and the same goes for Christianity if it is to be truly interpreted as a way of life, for decision is the stuff of which life is made.

In a well documented chapter[8] Herbert Waddams explains that decision is almost synonymous with the "will", so beloved by the classical writers. " 'Will' is personality in that aspect in which it comes to a decision to act in some way or other. It is the aspect of

8. *Life and Fire of Love* (S.P.C.K., 1964), pp. 18–32.

personality which gives direction by choice. Other aspects such as desire or thought are not exclusively acts of choice since they may come unbidden to the mind. But the will is the personality in the act of choosing, of self-determination."[9] But if will and choice are near synonyms there are good reasons for preferring the latter. In moral and ascetical theology the former word has taken on a grim and negative nuance; to the strong it becomes a restrictive task-master, and to the weak a matter for despair. To exercise "will-power" invariably means to resist temptation, to set the will on God or employ the will in prayer implies the tough acceptance of something unpleasant. Choice, decision denotes true freedom, it is a positive, wider and liberating notion.

How does one choose? The thorough-going existentialist must reply that there is no criterion, you must just choose, spontaneously and in the dark, so life is anguish or dread or anxiety. Atheistic existentialism is intensely pessimistic; can the Christian variety do any better? How does the Christian responsibly choose? The answer cannot be restricted to morality, for the simple reason that the vast majority of life's decisions are not moral ones at all: they transcend the ethical, as we shall see. If Christianity is a way of life, life most abundant, then it can depend on nothing less than that total and continuous relationship with God that we have called prayer. This in turn must depend on the way God acts upon us, the way he treats us if you like, and the way we respond. And this is enlightened for us by God's self-revelation in Christ, in the truths which are enshrined in the creed, but up-dated and put into usable terms. It is in this way that we shall discover how the doctrine of the Trinity becomes the very guide to life and decision.

This brings us to the all-important hyphen in our outline phrase *existential-ontological*. It is all-important because it safeguards us from the charge that we are rejecting the incontrovertible axiom of divine prevenience: God acts first, our prayer-relation starts from his side and comes to us in his self-revelation. Experience alone, or a thorough-going empiricism, cannot form the basis for my religion. The existential starting point has to be coupled with the ontological factor, the given, the creed. I am not St.

9. *Life and Fire of Love*, pp. 18–19.

Bernadette and I cannot claim her sort of experience. Faith in the creed is part of my present existence, so also is my membership of the community of faith, without which any sort of theology would be impossible. So Macquarrie firmly rejects the possibility of a purely existential theology[10] No man, primitive or sophisticated, can invent a personal religion based on his experience alone. However primitive or unformulated, religion has to start with revelation, with something from without, from God, to which a response of faith can be made. The only way to invent a private religion is to sit down and wait for a revelation; if and when it is disclosed, what follows ceases to be private. Moreover the first thing the recipient of revelation always does is to seek disciples to share it. I am committed to the revelation of God in Christ, the practical implications of which are crystallised in the creed. The creed is the given data corresponding to the ontological element in our definition. This approach, therefore, is existentially based in that it begins with human experience, with man, in fact with me, but it is not the kind of existentialism which ends with man. It is not humanism wherein man is be-all and end-all: the existential is hyphenated with -ontological.

So far the ontological has been vaguely described as the given, that which is set over against subjective experience; specifically as the creed which contains revealed truths, those which I am most unlikely to have discovered or worked out for myself, which I accept in faith. This is a reasonable interpretation because ontology means the study of "being", of that which simply *is*. This word is the crux of the whole book, and if we can but grasp its significance the rest should be more or less plain sailing. Again I am careful to use the pastoral-theological phrase: we are not concerned with the study of philosophy but with practical prayer.

In this way we can begin by saying that *beings* are simply *things*; every individual thing which makes up the world — trees, stars, animals, rocks — is a being. So the opposite of being, that which is not a being, is nothing: no-thing. In common speech we talk of a human being, a thing which is human. You can describe any particular being by enumerating its properties; an orange is a being which is reddish-yellow, round, juicy in the middle, pleasant

10. *Principles of Christian Theology*, p. 168.

to eat and three inches in diameter. Nothing is added to this description by saying that the orange *is*; on the other hand the description is nonsense if we conclude that the orange *is not*. Being is not the same as *a* being, neither is it a quality or property or characteristic of any particular being. It is rather a sort of overall *isness* in which all the beings participate by virtue that they are. All created things have being, but it is not a substance, or ground or tangible aspect of any of them. "When we talk of 'a being' or of 'the beings', we can mean anything at all that *is*: when we talk of 'Being' simply, we mean that character exemplified in all the beings, in virtue of which they *are* and stand out from nothing."[11]

The distinction which must be made clear at this point is that being is an existential, or dynamic concept. In other words being is distinct from, yet includes becoming. This is a difficult idea but it means that being, like the existent self, embraces both stability and activity, and is quite distinct from the idea of substance, or basic, static, thing-hood.[12]

Being is the incomparable that is wholly other to every particular being and comes before them. Being is the *transcendens* that is nevertheless nothing apart from the beings in which it is manifest. Being is not static but includes becoming and perhaps even has a history. Being takes the initiative in addressing man, in giving him speech, in setting him up in the light and openness. Being is gracious towards man and constitutes him its guardian.

As these descriptions of Being build up, we can hardly deny that for Heidegger, Being has something of a holy, divine character. Certainly, Heidegger does not identify Being with God, and yet I think it would be true to say that in his thought, Being has taken the place of God; for Being undoubtedly is furnished with most of the attributes that have been traditionally assigned to God, and Being seems to perform most of the functions that have belonged to God. Being is the incom-

11. *Martin Heidegger*, p. 61.
12. *Principles of Christian Theology*, pp. 97–105.

prehensible and wholly other that cannot be counted as an *ens creatum* and yet has more reality; Being both transcends the world and is immanent in it; Being is the author of revelation and grace.[13]

Very guardedly we must now ask *why* there are any beings? Even more guardedly, what is the "source" of being? For this is the first of all religious questions; crudely where and why *is* anything? The answer is Being, or Holy Being in Macquarrie's christianised sense of the word. But "source" implies "maker" of heaven and earth, with all its attendant difficulties. It makes God an object, *a* particular being — however great and exalted makes no difference — set over against the other beings. This is the central pastoral problem of God "out there", God above the bright blue sky. Macquarrie solves it by introducing another concept to which more attention must soon be paid. Instead of God (or Holy Being) understood as the source of, or maker, or creator, or first cause of the universe of beings, he speaks of God "letting-be". This phrase means not just leaving alone as in popular speech, but "enabling to be, empowering to be, or bringing into being".[14] This letting-be, moreover, is the essence of Being, not some external activity like making, or creating, but the outpouring, or self-giving of Being itself. "God's essence is Being, and Being, in turn, is letting-be. So it is of the essence of God to let-be. He does not, as it were, hoard Being within himself, and if he did, could we speak at all of God? We only call him 'God' and recognise him as holy Being, calling forth our worship, because he pours out being ..."[15] Phrases like outpouring and self-giving suggest love, love is letting-be, so God is love.

When we talk of "letting-be" we are to understand both parts of this hyphenated expression in a strong sense — "letting" as "empowering" and "be" as enjoying the maximal range of being that is open to the particular being concerned. Most typi-

13. *Martin Heidegger*, p. 57.
14. *Principles of Christian Theology*, p. 103.
15. *Principles of Christian Theology*, p. 183.

cally, "letting-be" means helping a person into the full realis-
ation of his potentialities for being; and the greatest love will be
costly, since it will be accomplished by the spending of one's
own being ... the very essence of God as Being is to let-be, to
confer, sustain, and perfect the being of the creatures.[16]

The outline of our new map takes shape in the form of a reinterpretation of the first succinct paragraph of the Apostles'
creed: I have faith in Being who lets-be the beings: God is Love.
This is the outline because all the rest of the creed elaborates it and
is contained within it.

The two words of our hyphenated starting point tie in together:
I live in this world and I believe in the creed. Or, I am an existent
being, and I am conscious, to some extent, of my being. I am also
conscious of the whole realm of being, of all the particular beings I
see, touch, hear, smell and taste. But through revelation, through
the gift of awareness, or spiritual sensitivity, or existence, or experience, or perhaps better, being-aliveness, I become aware not
only of the particular beings but of being itself. This is the initial
revelation or disclosure: what is revealed is being. This is the
ontological experience which makes me believe in the creed; it is
grace, or the gift of faith which grows out of my experience; it is a
general yet personal revelation which makes sense of the idea of a
special and repetitive revelation. I am made aware of being
through the particular beings which leads me to accept Being, or
Holy Being or God. Henceforth I shall follow Macquarrie in referring to God simply as Being, with the initial capital, but with all
the proviso and explication contained in his interpretation.[17]

There is still use for both maps: God as Being and God as
Father will illuminate one another, and they can be put together
by describing God as Personal Holy Being. Meanwhile the new
expression leads to some important practical issues. If revelation is
awareness of being, thence Being, through the beings, or in Macquarrie's phrase if being "is *present* and *manifest* in, with, and

16. *Principles of Christian Theology*, pp. 310–11.
17. *Principles of Christian Theology*, pp. 105–10.

D

through these particular beings",[18] then the essence of prayer *must* be relationship. It begins with a contemplative awareness rather than with acts of devotion isolated from experience. This experience, moreover, is sense-experience, or rather existential experience which contains the senses: experience and response with one's whole being. So there is substantiation for that strong, if neglected, strand in Christian spirituality which "seeks God in his creatures", and a further rejection for the Puritan quest for "pure spirit".

If our translated creed-outline sounds a little odd, and if we are using the concept of Being in a special way, there should be no devotional difficulty in associating the word with the Christian idea of God. The God of the Old Testament is "I am that I am", or "He who is", or as Macquarrie suggests "I cause to be" or even "I let-be what I let-be".[19] From that beginning ontology has played a central part in Christian theology. We shall soon see, if it is not clear already, that phrases like "Almighty Being" or "Supreme Being" are thoroughly unsatisfactory, even distortions, but it is the same word. So far as the emotive or psychological approach to prayer is concerned, the word is no startling innovation.

We must now fill in this outline, applying our basic frame of thought to the details contained within it.

18. *Principles of Christian Theology*, p. 80.
19. *Principles of Christian Theology*, pp.179–80.

FOUR

I and Me

I LIVE in this world and I believe in the creed. What do I mean by "I"? If I look back to my childhood I remember becoming aware of things, which we have now decided to call beings: my home, its garden, our dog, lawns, trees, flowers and so on. On a warm and fragrant summer evening I vividly remember gazing at a cherry tree and asking a pertinent question: why was the tree a tree, why was I me, and why was not the tree me and I it? What does it feel like to be a cherry tree? Would I like to be a cherry tree, or would I prefer to be me? This is an experience common to childhood and is in no way unusual; children are always personifying things and pretending to be other things. We shall see later that this experience is an elementary but genuine form of contemplation; in common with millions of other children I had experienced the *I-Thou* relation at about the same time as Martin Buber was so brilliantly explaining it.[1] I had also discovered something else, not only my "being" but also my "existence". In common with millions of other children I had discovered that I was an existentialist at about the same time as Martin Heidegger was explaining what that meant.

In one sense I was very close to the cherry tree, I got very near indeed to loving it, to being in harmony with it, happily contemplating it. But in another sense I stood out from it, I was different, I ex-isted. So:

... what differentiates a man from other beings in the world. The existentialists answer this question in terms of man's "existence", where the term "existence" is understood not in its traditional sense of whatever may be found occurring in the world,

1. *See* pp. 161–5 below.

but rather in its root sense of "standing out". In the traditional sense, men, cats, trees, and rocks all alike exist; but in the more restricted sense, while men, cats, trees, and rocks all *are*, only man is said to *exist* . . .

Men, cats, trees, rocks are *are*; they have being, we come across them in the world. But so far as we know, only man is open to his being, in the sense that he not only is, but is aware *that* he is, and aware too, in some degree, of *what* he is. He has his being disclosed to him, and this disclosure, as will be shown, comes not only in understanding but also over the whole range of his affective and conative existing in a world.[2]

This peculiarity of existence may be expressed in another way, by saying that man has a relation to himself. We continually use such expressions as "I hated myself for doing it", or "I feel pleased with myself", or even "I was not myself when I said that", and we understand well enough what is meant by these expressions, yet if we think about them, we see that they are something of a puzzle. Just who is the "I" that is distinguished from "myself"?[3]

This dilemma is to some extent resolved when I look again at my childhood. As I remember the little boy gazing at the cherry tree *I* am quite sure that it was *me*; there is a continuity between the boy looking at the tree and the man writing this book. But what is the relation between the two? What has happened in the meantime? For there is obviously a discontinuity as well; I am not the same "me" as the little boy in quite the way that the cherry tree is now the same cherry tree. I am not the same substantial self, or soul, or person, who just happens to have grown a bit and got a little older. The tree cannot help being the same tree, but I could have developed very differently; the tree could not possibly have turned into an oak or an elm, yet I could have become a doctor or an engineer instead of being a priest and a writer. I am not just a thing that has grown but an existential being who has developed

2. *Principles of Christian Theology*, p. 54.
3. *Principles of Christian Theology*, p. 55.

through struggle, circumstance and choice. And this makes looking back into the past rather frightening.

Then — as indeed now — certain possibilities and potentialities
were open to me, and between which I had to choose. Some of
these have been partially actualised; others have atrophied. I remember a learned aunt once telling me that I had "literary
hands", so I set about writing a novel at the age of about eight.
Since then I have written no novels but I have published quite a
lot of theology, such as it is. A little later my housemaster thought
that I was cut out for a brilliant academic career, but I was much
too interested in cricket and farming, and much too mentally lazy,
for that potential to come off. I might have married a particular
girl in my early twenties, but I did not; I married another lady
very much later. Now the only point of interest in this autobiography is that it is these choices, decisions and happenings,
actualised out of a far greater number of possibilities, that have
made "me". Although the "me" runs all through my life, and will
continue to do so, I am not some basic substance, self, or soul, to
which other things have been added. For a man-farmer to become
a priest (leaving aside any particular theology of ordination) is not
the same as a lump of clay becoming a jug; certain characteristics
like shape and colour being added to the same basic stuff. For to
be a farmer, or priest, or doctor, or lawyer is to give a specific
direction to total existence. It is a well known sociological fact that
work and vocation are formative of personal identity. "Throughout history, any particular work has been not only a means of
livelihood but also a source of self-identification ... to put it
simply, for most of history men have *been* what they *did*."[4] In
other words what *I* do and choose makes *me*. To look ahead a little
it follows that to *be* a Christian means much more than to believe
in certain credal propositions; it means a total faith-commitment
by which choice is exercised in a Christian way; it implies a contemplative or integrated outlook which creates a particular kind of
self. But let us return to Macquarrie and complete this existential
analysis by its -ontological counterpart.

"Existence fulfils itself in selfhood. An authentic self is a unitary,

4. Peter L. Berger, ed. *The Human Shape of Work* (Collier-Macmillan,
1964), p. 215.

stable, and relatively abiding structure in which the polarities of existence are held in balance and its potentialities are brought to fulfilment."[5] The boy gazing at the cherry tree was really "me". Nevertheless a self is a *relatively* abiding structure which cannot be regarded as a ready-made nature, or character, or soul, or collection of properties. It is something more fluid, active and experimental; an awareness, a potentiality, an involvement in life. a concern.

Objects in nature have their properties given to them, but what is "given" to man is an existence that stands before different possibilities of being, and among these it must responsibly discriminate. This brings us to a further point. Because selfhood is not a ready-made "nature", or collection of properties, but a potentiality that has to be responsibly actualised, man can either attain to authentic selfhood or miss it, and so fall below the kind of being that can properly be called "existence" in the fullest sense.[6]

Or further,

By a "person" we do not mean an invisible, intangible and immaterial soul-substance, but always an embodied self in the world. Not only is no purpose served by imagining a ghostly soul "inhabiting" the body, but the very idea is superfluous and confusing.[7]

In looking back on my life in the world as existence, or potentiality involving choice, I have so far given the impression that this is a fairly simple, easy-going business: certain possibilities are and one just chooses. Now two further factors of experience, or two aspects of one new factor, must be considered. Although I am conscious of responsible free will my choice is limited; at one stage I wanted to be Minister of Agriculture but I could not just choose to do that job, and had I struggled to attain to that position with

5. *Principles of Christian Theology*, p. 64.
6. *Principles of Christian Theology*, pp. 55–6.
7. *Principles of Christian Theology*, p. 65.

all my strength I doubt very much if I would have been successful. Apart from such obvious impossibilities, there is a strong sense that even in more reasonable, everyday decisions, I am subject to external forces, some benevolent and others malicious. Things just happen, they take a turn for the better, or worse, and my power of choice is restricted. When it is widened, or directed, by some benevolent external force or event I am apt to think in terms of "providence", which will be considered later. Seemingly malicious events might also be "providential", but there is also some sort of weakness, or frustration within myself which either makes me choose wrongly or, what is worse, undermines my power of decision altogether. I cannot make up my mind, either through lack of clarity on the issues involved, or through apathy, or through fear. Conversely, I find myself making decisions which I know to be the wrong ones, but I somehow cannot help it.

This is what Macquarrie calls the disorder of existence,[8] or to up-date and reinterpret old-map language, original and actual sin :"when we do look at actual human existing, we perceive a massive disorder in existence, a pathology that seems to extend all through existence, whether we consider the community or the individual, and that stultifies it. Because of this prevalent disorder, the potentialities of existence are not actualised as they might be, but are lost or stunted or distorted."[9]

In describing this disorder in existence, Macquarrie introduces some ideas which will be pertinent to our quest for a revivified Christian life through a new approach to prayer. "These disorders represent the retreat from possibility, decision-making, responsibility, individual liability and even from rationality. They move in the direction of a sub-human mode of being, that of the animal which is free from care and lives in and for its present."[10] After that it is no surprise to come across the old religious idea of "falling" — original and actual sin again — but more enlightening is the idea of "alienation", or "lostness".[11] Again we are in the

8. *Principles of Christian Theology*, pp. 59–64.
9. *Principles of Christian Theology*, pp. 59–60.
10. *Principles of Christian Theology*, p. 60.
11. *Principles of Christian Theology*, pp. 61–4.

realm of convention; sin is separation from God, not to be "saved"
is to be "lost", but here there are special implications.

> The basic alienation is really from oneself, in the full range of
> one's possibility and facticity. This in turn leads to alienation
> from other existents, for, as we have seen, individualism at one
> extreme and collectivism at the other take the place of authentic
> community. Is it not the case, however, that there is still a third
> level of alienation, a deeper level where one feels alienated from
> the whole scheme of things? Perhaps this could be called "lost-
> ness". It is the sense of being cut off not only from one's own
> true being or from the being of others, but from all being, so
> that one has no "place" in the world. This is surely the deepest
> despair that can arise out of the disorder of existence . . . What
> is distinctive in sin, however, is the last point to which we came
> in our discussion of models of human disorder — the notion of
> "lostness", of being alienated not only from oneself and from
> other existents but, at a still deeper level, from all being. The
> religious man would say that this lostness is separation from
> God . . .[12]

It will suffice to note here that the opposite of sin is harmony, or
integration, or balance, which is again close to contemplation, or
contemplative awareness, of oneself, one's place in creation and
one's relation with God. In turn this is what we call prayer, and
what the Old Testament means by "righteousness".

I live in this world and I believe in the creed. I begin in existential fashion with my own experience and go to Macquarrie to make
some sense of it. And I started this particular quest by referring
back to my childhood — by no means childish — relation with
a cherry tree, which helped to sort out the relation between *I* and
me. I emerged as a self, or human existent, or existential being, the
fundamental character of which was not some fixed substantial
soul but a potentiality for becoming a self, or more and more of an
authentic self. This is still the case for existence "is never complete
in its being. To exist is always to be on the way, so that one can
never, as it were, pin down the existent at any precise moment and

12. *Principles of Christian Theology*, p. 62.

give an exhaustive description. He is constituted by possibilities rather than properties."[13] I live in this world inevitably begins with looking back at the past, and onwards into the future: I have discovered time, or rather temporality, for "It is temporality, with its three dimensions of past, present, and future that makes the kind of being called 'existence' possible."[14] Or "What constitutes existence or personal being is a peculiar and complex temporal nexus in which the three dimensions of past, present, and future are brought into a unity . . . Authentic selfhood implies the attaining of a unified existence."[15]

But temporality is a substantive word, which Macquarrie translates as *commitment*, which looks to the future, and *acceptance*, which is retrospective and which has produced the present: the authentic "moment" of the existentialist philosophers.[16] In the homeliest language, while there's life there's hope and its no use crying over spilt milk. Acceptance is very near to what moral theology calls humility, an honest facing of the facts of a situation, a recognition of one's limitation, finitude and facticity. This includes, and is overshadowed by the fact of death, which as any Christian ought to know but frequently pushes aside, is a *positive* fact of human being. It is death which can bring perspective and a joyful seriousness into life, and which ultimately points beyond being to Being.[17] We have become hopelessly morbid about death, we will not accept it, which is a serious hindrance to the development of spirituality on any level. I remain grateful to a conscientious nursemaid who dutifully pointed out that certain berries in the garden were poisonous, adding — I suspect through an over zealous interpretation of Genesis 3 — that were I but to touch them I would surely die. Of course I touched them, and spent a vivid twenty-four hours looking at my beloved cherry tree and awaiting death. I am still no spiritual genius but it helped.

13. *Martin Heidegger*, pp. 12–13.
14. *Principles of Christian Theology*, p. 66.
15. *Principles of Christian Theology*, p. 67.
16. *Principles of Christian Theology*, pp. 67–8.
17. *Principles of Christian Theology*, pp. 69–70.

To what am I committed? First to being in its presence and manifestation, as Macquarrie puts it, and which began with the cherry tree. But being becomes Being: genuine commitment is an existential attitude directed to what Macquarrie calls some master possibility.[18] This is my faith in the creed, as a guide and interpreter of life through prayer as relationship. I try to accept that my experience includes frustration, anxiety, facticity, limitation, and that it depends very largely on extraneous forces: "providence", or "grace", or "judgment", or Something. And it will end in death. Can the Christian creed make sense of this, or must I side with the Sartrean philosophers and write it all off as absurd? I choose the former — with prayer as its key — and the time has come to look at some of the practical implications which arise out of this new interpretation.

First, there is a good deal of enlightenment for several aspects of traditional spirituality. Providence, grace and judgment have arisen out of living experience not out of the text-book. Original and actual sin, concepts seemingly so foreign to the modern mind, have also acquired existential status. Sin as falling, imbalance, alienation, lostness, disharmony, is in line with, yet more enlightening than, traditional and devotional treatment. We have also seen that the existential attitude of acceptance makes very good sense of the virtue of humility, lifting it out of the negative devotional realm into that of purposeful activity. Moreover, as Macquarrie shows,[19] the failure to accept facticity and finitude issues either in pride or sloth, which in turn resolves itself into lust and gluttony. It would not be difficult to formulate the classical list of the capital sins out of our premise — I live in the world — examined from an existential-ontological viewpoint. The difference is that this classic list becomes experienced fact rather than an academic catalogue. We have also seen, over and over again, how, in one sense or another, contemplation is fundamental to ordinary, healthy human existence. We shall have to examine this carefully, but suffice it to say at this point that we are not dealing with some esoteric attainment of "advanced" religion.

Finally, faith is commitment to some master concern — "not a

18. *Principles of Christian Theology*, pp. 68–9.
19. *Principles of Christian Theology*, pp. 60–61.

mere belief but an existential attitude" — revealed, given and accepted. All the old arguments about faith and belief, conation and cognition, no doubt served their times well enough, but our existential-ontological analysis has made them superfluous. Soon we shall look at the content of Christian faith in more detail, to try to discover precisely how this life-commitment works out in practice; how, through prayer-as-relation, it interprets, integrates, unifies, and generally makes sense of human life.

But secondly, there are certain conflicts with devotional tradition thrown up by our examination of "I" and "me" on the new map. The most fundamental of these is at the very centre of traditional ascetical theology: there seems to be something unsatisfactory about the usual view of spiritual progress. The textbook version consists in the eradication of sin and the cultivation of the virtues. So far so good, but the implicit model behind this process is the substantial soul, or soul-substance; some kind of human "thing", which has fallen, which has been offered redemption, and plods on towards salvation. Perhaps it was only the medieval peasant who thought of the soul as a physical organ situated somewhere between the brain and the heart, but so long as this kind of symbol prevails the most sophisticated can hardly avoid something very like it. To speak of a spiritual substance gets us nowhere, and the traditional vocabulary of devotion does not help: the soul gets "stained" by sin and "nourished" by grace, not to mention having virtue "infused" into it.

Perhaps a more common devotional model derives from an over literal interpretation of Genesis 2: 7. The soul, or self, becomes a semi-animated statue, a puppet, which tends to get corroded and encrusted with grime — "stained" by venial sin — and which might develop a few more serious cracks — mortal sin. The grime has to be scrubbed off, the rotten parts chiselled out and the cracks made good, until, with constant devotional polishing, the statue is restored to its pristine beauty. Perfection comes very close to getting back to where we started, standing happily on a pedestal in the garden of Eden. The classical Three Ways of progress also tend to this view; first purgation, washing off the grime; then illumination, polishing up the stone; then union, back in Eden.

This is a parody of traditional teaching but the idea persists. To the classic writers perfection is a more sophisticated concept, and they go out of their way to explain the Three Ways as an analytic scheme, the boundaries of which blur and overlap. The existential concept of time, with the three dimensions of past, present and future brought into a unity, makes still more sense of this classical progression. Nevertheless, parody or no, the weaknesses are there. Macquarrie warns that "the idea of a substantial self that gets inserted or implanted into the body at the beginning of life suggests something ready-made that has only to grow as, let us say, the organs of the body do".[20] And that is a mistake I made in *Christian Proficiency*, and even more blatantly in *Pastoral Theology: a Reorientation*.[21] There it was explained that the *regula*, based on trinitarian doctrine, brought all the divine attributes into prayer and life, guarded against spiritual errors and generally kept the "soul" healthy and vigorous, consequently it was bound to "grow". I backed up this argument with what now looks like a false analogy; you cannot, purposefully, make a child grow, you can only keep him healthy and leave the growth to God: so with the "soul". I am still reluctant to throw over this classical scheme, it contains profound truth, and it still works out in practice for those who are able to embrace it. But I think these are becoming fewer, and we must be bold enough to subject this ancient and venerable map to honest criticism, not because it is wrong, but because it might be out-of-date. There is a chance, moreover, that the new map might enlighten the old: the divine office was once seen to "link the soul with God" so many times a day, it was a "tuning in" to the continuous heavenly doxology, it "kept the soul afloat", and even sanctified the day. These old devotional ideas no longer command much respect, but if the office is seen to be a focus or concentrate of everyday experience of divine and Holy Being the whole thing looks different.

If we begin not with a ready-made soul-substance, a fixed entity, but with a potentiality for becoming a self, "spiritual progress" undergoes a remarkable transformation. The old idea of

20. *Principles of Christian Theology*, p. 66.
21. *See* pp. 192–247.

"making your soul" becomes pregnant with new meaning, for it no longer implies a cleansing and polishing up exactly what it says: construction out of potential, the attaining of unified existence, the creative movement towards authentic selfhood. This is achieved by choice and decision; ideas which also undergo important changes of emphasis. Traditionally, choice is subjected to two unfortunate connotations. It is either negated to mean a regrettable fact of fallen life, something that one should never have to face, or it is narrowed to the merely moral, to mean practically the same as temptation. On the new map choice is broadly positive; it is the very stuff of life, the raw material out of which authentic selfhood is made. Not just resistance to temptation, not tuning-in techniques of prayer, not meditative acts of devotion, but the ability, strength and courage to choose, must lie at the heart of any contemporary spiritual theology. Acts, meditation, and above all contemplative awareness of Holy Being, all remain within the Christian life of prayer, but they are directed away from the protection of the soul's health towards discernment of the will of God in particular situations, thence to bold and courageous choice.

Choice implies risk, outgoing and self-forgetful risk,[22] which is an essential but overlooked "attribute" of God himself. It is also at the heart of the Gospel for it implies looking beyond the limits of oneself for life's "master concern".[23] Playing safe, the principle behind rigorist ethics, is self condemned, while old-fashioned probabilism takes on a much more positive and up-to-date look. It used to say something to the effect that when in doubt you could act according to a degree of probability without committing sin: now it says risk and make your soul. This is not to advocate foolhardiness, and certainly not to excuse sin, for the way of decision requires greater spiritual responsibility, more developed powers of discernment, than ever before.

We may sum up by taking another critical look at the old ideal which is the basis of the Anglican Prayer Book, and thence of conventional spirituality which still prevails, albeit under some

22. *Principles of Christian Theology*, p. 183.
23. *Principles of Christian Theology*, p. 69.

duress. And at first we face a dilemma. If our new ideal is integration, or balance, or contemplative harmony, within the authentic self, within community, with the natural environment and finally with Being, or God, then Benedictinism fits exactly: it is as contemporary as today's newspaper. Even its foundation in poverty and chastity make a good deal of sense, for the first puts love of creation over ownership and the second love of neighbour over exploitation. It is when we look at the detailed method that things are different. It is difficult to avoid the impression that stability within the monastery is the ideal setting for the cleansing and polishing of the stable soul, and the *regula* becomes geared to this process. It is silly to interpret monasticism as irresponsible flight from the world, yet could it be tinged with the "illusory security" of which Macquarrie speaks[24] and which is ultimately associated with the soul-substance idea? The monastery is no bed of cotton wool, no escape from reality, but it is a good place to house the soul for the cleaning and polishing operation. If there is contemporary significance of poverty and chastity what are we to make of obedience? Let us eschew the childishness that accuses monks of irresponsibility, of running away from the problems and pressures of life, yet the vow of obedience is a wonderful way of polishing the statue, but hardly the method of making your soul by choice? It is compatible with the divine risk involved in the attainment of authentic, integrated selfhood?

Existence "can either choose itself or lose itself; it can either exist (stand out) as the distinctive being that it is, or it can be submerged in a kind of anonymous routine manner of life, in which its possibilities are taken over and dictated to it by circumstances or by social pressures".[25] Existence is always personal and yet always "being-in-the-world" and "being-with-others". The individual-corporate, and obedience-responsibility, relations are as pendulums that have swung from side to side throughout Christian history, but the tradition of our immediate past has been more than a little overweighted on the obedience-corporate side.

The easiest thing in the world is to swing too far, but certain

24. *Principles of Christian Theology*, p. 69.
25. *Martin Heidegger*, p. 14.

fundamental points have now arisen from this examination of the first part of my premise — I live in this world — I exist. We must now proceed to examine the ontological basis of my life as interpreted and guided by prayer: — and I have faith in the creed.

PART TWO

. . . And I believe in the creed

FIVE

Triune Being

THE DOCTRINE of the Trinity is just about the most practical idea that the Church has ever come up with. It is the creed in embryo, the foundation of prayer, and the guide to decision. Like all true theology, the doctrine of the Trinity is rooted in experience, and it safeguards the dynamic as against the static idea of God.

This practicality of the doctrine should not be surprising — although it probably is — because something very like it has arisen out of my analysis of ordinary experience. I have spoken of some external power which both guides and limits my choice, of sudden events over which I have no control. I have referred to this as providence, as grace and judgment, external to me and transcending me, sometimes it gives me a sense of harmony or happy adjustment, sometimes of alienation and frustration. My experience with the cherry tree was not something I sought, it happened, and the same sort of thing continues to happen. Nevertheless I am not entirely dependent on these outside forces, I can accept or reject the experience of harmony, or love for created things, and to some extent I can seek it by co-operating with grace. And the cherry tree itself acts as a mediator between the external power of grace and my response to it; sometimes I am at one with the tree, sometimes I stand out from it, ex-isting. The tree mediates between my being and Being which lets-be.

This experience is very primitive. Ancient peoples were frightened of the thunder, of some noisy and terrifying power that had to be propitiated. They were also conscious of benevolent immanence, of soft and comfortable fertility. They knew of transcendent grace, gentle rain and sunshine, and of malevolent immanence, disease, pain and the demonic. They needed a mediator and invented one in the form of the totem, or sacred tree: perhaps a cherry tree?

St. Augustine worked it out in psychological terms. To be made in the image of God meant to be trinitarian in structure: mind-knowledge-love; memory-intellect-will; sense-thought-spirit. In my most elementary experience I feel things, I think about things, and I sense things by the subtler ways of beauty and love. Yet I am equally convinced that I am a unity, I am one being not three. This Trinity continues to impinge upon my active experience. There are anxieties about which I can do nothing; the sickness of a friend, the threat of war or other disaster, sudden personal tragedy, against which I can only trust in providence. Nevertheless "only" is not quite the Christian word, for providence is neither fate nor luck. There are even more frightening challenges in which I am far *too* responsible, too much depends on me: the important interview, the critical decision. Here the need is not for trust in providence but for inspiration, guidance and spiritual support. And since I believe in the creed, these two types of experience are somehow linked up with Christ the mediator; Christ who points to the Father and sends the Spirit. Life is ruled by trinitarian experiences of this kind, so it should not be surprising that life is ruled and made sense of by a Triune God.

The old map of the Trinity abounds in theological and devotional insights of inexhaustible richness. Joachim Jeremias seems unable to stop finding ever-new depths of meaning in the single word *Abba* — Father, so constantly on the lips of Jesus. We call Jesus the Son of God because that is exactly who he is, and if you search for a short telling phrase to describe the ever-present divine immanence it would be hard to improve on Holy Spirit. Nevertheless this language has serious shortcomings, especially in modern context. Like so much traditional symbolism it presents a curious combination of naïvety and sophistication, and there is need for a mediatorial language to marry the two. The new language of being supplies this need, not supplanting the old but leading up to, and illuminating it.

The old creeds were most carefully designed to guard against tri-theism, insisting upon the unity of the one God, yet in devotion and liturgy this error still persists. To the intelligent inquirer the recurring refrain "Glory be to the Father, *and* to the Son, *and* to the Holy Ghost" must give the impression that three gods, or at least three separate things, are being worshipped, one after the other. The formula may invite intellectual meditation but not a simple contemplative grasp. Ideally, so we are instructed, all Christian prayer is trinitarian, offered to the Father, through the Son, in and by the Spirit. Yet in practice prayers of praise and adoration tend to be directed to the transcendent Father; personal petition, meditation and intercession depend primarily upon the indwelling Spirit; while the eucharist and affective devotion becomes concentrated on Jesus Christ. By perseverance over the years, this pattern induces a recollective state of contemplative awareness; the three modes or aspects fuse into a unity, yet the weakness of this scheme of things is everywhere admitted.

A further difficulty is that the old maps are written in static terms. Despite the essential dynamism of the Trinity the creed speaks of "substance" and "person" in the old ready-made-statue image. It hardly helps to be told that the word "substance" has created difficulties since the Council of Nicaea, and that "person" is an unfortunate translation of the Greek *hypostasis* or the Latin *persona*.[1] Even the theologically educated are hard put to avoid a picture of the Trinity as a united family of one blood-substance, sitting in a posed group and gazing back at them at prayer. The map clearly states that the Son "sitteth on the right hand of God the Father Almighty", so presumably the Holy Ghost sitteth on his left?

If I wished to visit the county town of Devonshire, and my map called the place, quite correctly, Exoniensis, or just as correctly, Isca Dumnoniorum, I might reasonably expect a little confusion on the way, especially were I to inquire of the local inhabitants. Devonian common sense might insinuate that if I wanted to go to Exeter why could not I have said so in the first place? If my map called it something else perhaps I should think about getting a newer one? This is exactly what I shall do, retaining the old for reference and for liturgy.

1. *Principles of Christian Theology*, pp. 174–8.

On the new map God is Holy Being, or simply Being, but he is also triune Being.

The Father may be called "primordial" Being. This expression is meant to point to the ultimate act or energy of letting-be, the condition that there should be anything whatsoever, the source not only of whatever is but of all possibilities of being . . . We do not then think of primordial Being in isolation as an "uncarved block" or whatever, but as a source of outpouring which is inseparable from the whole structure of Being and which is something like a "movement" within it. To think triune Being, we must hold as fast to the unity as to the trinity. The Father, as primordial Being, is the depth of the mystery of God. We could not possibly know anything of him "in himself", we know him only in so far as he does pour himself out in the dynamics of Being and is revealed in and through the other persons who are joined with him in the unity of Being.

The second person of the Trinity, the Son, we shall call "expressive" Being. The energy of primordial Being is poured out through expressive Being and gives rise to the world of particular beings, having an intelligible structure and disposed in space and time. Being mediates itself to us through the beings. These beings, as we say, come into being and pass out of being, that is to say, they have a temporal character, so that Being (and certainly any dynamic Being) is understood by us in terms of time. In identifying the second person of the Trinity with expressive Being, we remember of course that the Son, in Christian theology, is also the Word, or Logos, the agent of the Father in the creation of the world as well as in its recreation. The Logos is expressive Being, that is to say, it is not to be identified with the beings through which it gains expression. Thus we say that the Logos, or second person, is "generated" by the Father or is "of one substance" (consubstantial) with the Father. In saying this, we assign the Logos to the side of Being, rather than to the side of the beings. However, the Logos expresses itself in the beings, or rather, the Logos expresses Being in the beings. The primordial Being of the Father, which would otherwise be entirely hidden, flows out through expressive

Being to find its expression in the world of beings. Christians believe that the Father's Being finds expression above all in the finite being of Jesus, and in such a way that his being is caught up into Being itself.[2]

Of the third person of the Trinity

We may designate him "unitive" Being, for it is in the "unity of the Holy Ghost" that the Church in her liturgy ascribes glory to the Father and the Son, and, more generally, it is the function of the Spirit to maintain, strengthen and, where need be, restore the unity of Being with the beings, a unity which is constantly threatened.[3]

The best way to understand a map is to use it, and the surest test of its accuracy is safe arrival at one's destination. Here we must remain content with plotting our course, and already certain advantages of the new map are apparent.

On the old map the doctrine of creation was separated, or at least separable, from the doctrine of God: first there was God, secondly he made the world. On the new map these doctrines merge into one:

God's essence is Being, and Being, in turn is letting-be. So it is of the essence of God to let-be. He does not, as it were, hoard Being within himself, and if he did, could we speak at all of God? We only call him "God" and recognize him as holy Being, calling forth our worship, because he pours out Being, moving out from primordial through expressive Being. Of this, more will be said when we come to the doctrine of creation.[4] For the present, however, we can already see that as Being moves out to manifest itself in the world of beings, it involves itself in what can only be called "risk". What constitutes Being as God, as holy Being that gives itself and demands our allegiance, is precisely that it does not gather itself together as pure immutable Being but that

2. *Principles of Christian Theology*, pp. 182–3.
3. *Principles of Christian Theology*, p. 184.
4. *Principles of Christian Theology*, pp. 209–14.

it goes out into the openness of a world of beings, a world of change and multiplicity and possibility. We talk of "risk" because in this process Being could become split, fragmented, and torn within itself. The risk becomes acute when the universe brings forth beings, such as man, who have responsibility and a limited freedom that empowers them up to a point to manage their own lives and even to manipulate nature.[5]

The risk of letting-be, or outpouring of Being, or self-giving, obviously points to love, so Being, letting-be, creation and love become almost synonyms: Being lets-be the beings — God is love.

This supports my interpretation of prayer as relationship, old-style habitual recollection, and only secondarily as specific acts, foci, or concentrates, of that relationship. As I. T. Ramsey has well expounded, the basis of spirituality is not psychological but ontological,[6] it begins not with a search for God but with response to our being grasped, or let-be, by him; the relationship which is prayer is not forged by acts, it *is*.

There is further support for that orthodox but nevertheless suspect type of spirituality which is based on creation: "seing God in creatures". In spite of Augustine, Irenaeus, Justin Martyr, Hugh of St. Victor, Francis of Assisi, Thomas Aquinas, Julian of Norwich, Thomas Traherne, and hundreds more, the Church has remained uncomfortable about this approach.[7] It smacks of natural religion as contrary to the Christian revelation, as the substitution of a sentimental aesthetic for true faith, as pantheistic and sensuous: spirituality grows in detachment from creatures. Could this suspicion derive from the old-style trinitarian formula? And does the new formula make more sense?

Returning to my cherry tree, which I take to be my initial experience of being in its presence and manifestation, my first, but oft-repeated "spiritual experience", then the old-map interpretation is, to say the least, incredibly complicated. I have described

5. *Principles of Christian Theology*, pp. 183–4.
6. *Theology for Today* in *Spirituality for Today*, ed. E. James (S.C.M., 1967), p. 75.
7. *See* Chapter 12 below.

this experience as subjectively trinitarian — body, mind, spirit. I saw the tree, I thought about it, I was somehow moved, inspired, stirred up by it. And I believe in the creed: what does it all mean? God the Father made it: how? when? by what mysterious natural cycle? Is he still concerned about it? Or is he immutable, transcendent, other from it, away from it, above it? Let us try God the Son. He is Redeemer, not only of people but of the universe, dying on a cross, a wooden cross, cherry wood? Does Christ redeem my tree? Irenaeus and others hint that he might: "the whole creation groaneth and travaileth in pain together until now."[8] Does Jesus really care for my tree? The old devotional catechism says that God is above, God is around, God is within. The Holy Ghost is immanent, is he *in* the tree? Can I worship the tree because God is in it? Is it a sacred tree? Horrors, that can't be right: God is spirit.

The old map is too small. What of the larger scale *Quicunque Vult*? This insists, by punching the point home over and over again, that the three persons are interdependently one God: the Father is immanent and the Holy Ghost transcendent. Perhaps God the Father is in the tree? Constant study of this formula, curious and comic as it may sound to modern ears, ultimately illuminates the experience of God as Trinity in Unity, but the intricacies are enormous and the dangers terrifying. If I stick to One God then Son and Spirit become subservient to the Father, which is monarchianism, or adoptionism, or something equally sinister. If I insist on the trinity of persons, albeit of one substance, then I am courting tri-theism, or modalism, or Sabellianism or some such lethal subtlety. It hardly helps to interpret my experience of a cherry tree, it is all somewhat removed from life.

Optimistically assuming that I steer my way through this maze, all I can hope for is a discursive and academic meditation about the tree and its relation to me and to God. I may be avoiding heresy but I am a long way from bringing trinitarian depth and richness into everyday experience. To achieve that, to bring God into life, to give the Trinity existential significance, I must sum up

8. Romans 8: 22.

all this theological speculation in a single contemplative glance. I must see the tree in the Trinity, unite with it, love it, enter into harmony with it and through it, in God, with the universe it symbolises.

On the new map the tree is a being, it *is* because God lets-it-be. It is there by the outpouring of primordial Being through express-ive Being, so it verily participates in Being; unitive Being brings into unity and maintains in unity this particular being with Being. In the tree Being is expressed as presence and manifestation, and all this applies to me too. God lets-me-be; I am one with the tree, participating in Being: God is still transcendent, still immanent, still the Redeemer of the universe, but more than anything he is All in all.

What a transformation; what glory in stark simplicity. God is no longer an object set over against creation, yet creation is abso-lutely dependent on him. Experience is no longer a discursive meditation winding its way through a maze of theological intri-cacy but a single contemplative glance, a unitive harmony of me, beings and Being. The spiritual journey that starts from here may be not entirely without danger, but it is no tight-rope walk over yawning chasms of heresy. If there is risk, then it is part of love, of the outpouring of Being: risk is a divine attribute.

The Church insists that God's creation is very good, then hedges it about with safeguards, provisos, and cautionary tales. There is a proper Christian asceticism, a true poverty which excludes the selfish exploitation of nature, but I do not need a list of deistic rules about how to treat trees. I want to bring harmony into myself by loving them, and so achieve harmony with God. The symbol of Father-creator, and of Jesus, Redeemer-Son, inspires devotion and faith, but in everyday living it is Triune Being that guides experience. One point must be added. A cherry tree is a beautiful thing, a steel pylon carrying power through the valley has a grace of its own but it appeals to me differently, a rusty tin-shed has no grace of any sort, but substitute any one for any other and the result is exactly the same. Primordial-expressive-unitive Being lets-be the beings: God is love.

If prayer starts here, with the awareness of being, with accept-ance and commitment, with response to Being in grace and judgment, it becomes concentrated into specific acts. Contemplative harmony, even on this lowly level, is comparatively rare, and although it is the beginning of prayer, the concentrate or focus is still necessary. The new map helps here too. What do I do when I "say my prayers"?

I used to kneel in chapel, or elsewhere, and "recollect the presence of God" or "invoke the Holy Spirit". I thought of the divine omnipresence, God is everywhere, a comforting if bald theological statement. I thought of the divine immanence, of the Holy Ghost indwelling, of the Paraclete, the Comforter, the Inspirer of prayer within the depths of my soul, perhaps getting "infused" into it and "nourishing" it. I could meditate on this for hours, without saying any prayers, but even with my comparatively advanced theological education (or perhaps because of it) it was a difficult and frustrating business. I could try to contemplate the indwelling Spirit with a blank mind, as it were, which frequently put me in the mood for prayer, although the distinction between the inspiration of the Holy Ghost and my distracted day-dreams remained remarkably thin. However I eventually said some prayers.

Prayers of praise brought the transcendental concepts into my total life, but how, precisely, does one "offer prayer to the Father"? It is difficult to avoid some idea of an objective, substantial things, or Person; God as object among objects, a Being among beings, God "out there". However sophisticated the symbol, this error is difficult to avoid. I have argued that the symbol is not very important so long as we realise that it *is* a symbol and that we know what we are doing, but it remains a technical error. I have resorted to the neo-classical "open-space" symbol, in in which prayer is offered to the Father, transcendent and inscrutable, and therefore unsymbolised, through an open space. This is an idea that seems to lie behind some modern liturgical architecture; my vivid impression of the Roman Catholic cathedral in Liverpool is that prayer and praise rise to the Father through the central tunnel or "chimney". This is a sophisticated symbol, or non-symbol, yet it does not really solve the problem; it is still a subject-object relation, and can such an inscrutable, incomprehensible God properly be called Father?

Old and new maps link up here, for Father means Personal Being.

Prayer and meditation related to the Son present greater difficulties, which are known well enough. Here there is no question of anthropomorphism, for Jesus *is* truly man, not just "personal"; he is the supreme and ultimate "symbol" of God, we need no other. But what is meant by his presence? Do we, with St. Ignatius Loyola, imagine Christ as present yet invisible? If so, is such devotion real and meaningful to modern people? Or do we settle for some vague, all-enveloping "humanity" without body parts, or passions? If so can we truly talk of Jesus Christ, can we talk *to* Jesus Christ, who was conceived by the Holy Ghost and born of the Virgin Mary?

The new map cuts clean through this theological jungle. Now I simply "sink into Being", which is no esoteric technique, no forced devotional exercise, but a concentrate of life which is trinitarian. To think that the Father made me, the Son redeemed me, and the Holy Ghost inspires me; that God is "above", "around", and "within": now this is all summed-up, concentrated, simplified in the experience that Being lets-be. Indeed this new language needs to be pondered and grasped but once this is achieved one has only to surrender. If need be I look at something, a being, like me, and this manifests the Trinity: primordial-expressive-unitive Being; creation-redemption-consummation, at a single contemplative glance. Or perhaps Being is like an ocean of reality upon which one floats rather than sinks into? It is a simple uncomplicated surrender, but an active surrender of oneself into the whirl of divine activity.

Or perhaps the difference between the old and new approach is analogous to that between preparing to drive a car and boarding a jet. The first calls for a concentrated tenseness, working out a series of discursive acts; brake off, clutch in, first gear, look in mirror, carefully now, off we go, but concentrate: recollect the Almighty Father, imagine the present Christ, pray to the Spirit, tense the spiritual muscles, ready, steady, pray. Or board the jet, faithfully conscious of its complex power, and sink, surrender.

"Glory be to the Father, and to the Son, and to the Holy Ghost" remains important to both devotion and liturgy; the new

map introduces, implements, and illuminates, but does not super-
sede the old. Yet I make bold to suggest two alternatives, one very
ancient and one very new: Holy-Holy-Holy — Let-be, Let-be,
Let-be.

SIX

Triune Activity

THE IDEA prevails that God made the world, once upon a time, and that it was very good. Then at some later date came the Fall, things went wrong through the rebellion of Satan and Adam. Taken by surprise, God had to work out some way of putting things to rights: in the beginning was the Word, who was to become incarnate, suffer, die, rise again, ascend into heaven, and thus redeem, or offer redemption to (according to which atonement theory one adopts) the fallen universe. The present task is to press on towards the final consummation in glory, which, like the person-statue, looks very much like a return to square one; back in Eden where it all started.

That is parody, yet it sets out a viewpoint which is not confined to popular devotion but which crops up from time to time in serious historical theology. In the Middle Ages, Duns Scotus and the Franciscans fought the Thomists about whether the incarnation would have taken place irrespective of the Fall. The argument sounds absurdly academic yet we must take the Scotist side on grounds of the most practical importance. The centre of theism is the relation between God and the world, and the incarnation is its end-point: "God, we may say, is so intimately involved with his creation that in a remarkable way Creator and creature become one in the incarnation."[1] So prayer is primarily relation, not a series of acts, and Christian prayer is trinitarian because, although natural religion gropes after this idea, only Christ fully reveals it.

The dangers and complexities inherent in my parody are overcome when this doctrine is reinterpreted by the new language:

1. *Principles of Christian Theology*, p. 203.

Creation involves risk, and this risk in turn issues in sin and evil which threatens the creatures with dissolution and distortion. ... Creation, involving risk, passes without interruption into providence, whereby the threat of dissolution is continually being overcome. Providence, in turn, is continuous with reconciliation; or, to express it in another way, reconciliation is the highest providential activity of God. By "reconciliation" is meant the activity whereby the disorders of existence are healed, its imbalances redressed, its alienations bridged over. Reconciliation in turn is continuous with consummation, the bringing of creation to its perfection. Creation, reconciliation, and consummation are not three successive activities of God, still less could we think that he has to engage in reconciliation because creation was unsuccessful. The three indeed are represented successively in the narrative presentation of the Christian faith, but theologically they must be seen as three moments in God's great unitary action. Creation, reconciliation, and consummation are not separate acts but only distinguishable aspects of one awe-inspiring movement of God, his love or letting-be, whereby he confers, sustains, and perfects the being of the creatures. ... It is not that at a given moment God adds the activity of reconciliation to his previous activities, or that we can set a time when his reconciling activity began. Rather, it is the case that at a given time there was a new and decisive revelation of an activity that had always been going on, an activity that is equiprimordial with creation itself.[2]

How does this help in prayer and practice? How do I experience this three-fold divine activity? And how does it guide my everyday choice?

God the Father, primordial Being, Love who outpours himself in letting-be, acts by way of *transcendent providence*, for "The assertion of God's providence is just another way of asserting his constant creating and sustaining energy."[3] Further:

2. *Principles of Christian Theology*, pp. 246–7.
3. *Principles of Christian Theology*, p. 219.

Belief in providence, like belief in creation itself, is founded existentially. It is through happenings that increase and strengthen our being — that do so not because of our own efforts primarily, but sometimes even in spite of our own efforts — that we come to believe in providence; and we do so because in these happenings we have become aware of the presence of Being, acting on us and in us.[4]

It should also be said that the belief in providence that is developed in the Bible is a mature and adult belief. It is very far from a groundless optimism (this is more characteristic of humanism) or any infantile belief that the universe ought to be ordered to fit in with one's own ego-centred desires and ambitions. The Hebrew prophets' belief in providence was not just a belief in divine favours, or a belief that everything must turn out well for Israel in the end. It was belief in an ordering of history by a God who is holy and righteous as well as merciful, so that his providence might be experienced as a discipline, and indeed the prophets have as much to say about God's judgment of Israel as about his favour.[5]

God the Son, expressive Being, incarnate in Jesus Christ, reveals the way of *sacrificial faith-commitment*, which cannot be better expressed than by the devotional idea that Jesus offers final succour while making absolute demand. And Jesus reveals both an ethic and a "way of life" which is wider and deeper than morality.

The Holy Ghost, unitive Being, strives to maintain and strengthen the unity of Being with the beings, or God with me. In the concrete situation he *inspires discernment* into both providential activity and into the mind of Christ.

God the Holy Trinity, therefore, impinges on my life in this three-fold way: *providence-sacrifice-discernment*; or transcendence-mediation-immanence; or providence-ethic-inspiration. Ideally these trinities fuse into a unity, so that the saints follow the will of God spontaneously; the mind of Christ is in-

4. *Principles of Christian Theology*, p. 220.
5. *Principles of Christian Theology*, pp. 222–3.

tuitively read into the providential situation: they grasp its significance and *know* what to do next. But lesser men frequently do not, so we are forced to analyse in order to respond and choose, or better still in order more closely to approximate, over the years, to the saintly ideal.

So every significant situation must first be examined in the light of providence. What is God doing? What is he trying to get across in *this* situation? More commonly, why has this happened to me? Why has God done this to me? The tragedy is that this last question is usually asked in a spirit of frustration, but if the attitude could be changed into one of adventurous inquiry it becomes not only legitimate but a very good question indeed. In other words, what am I in this particular situation for? What are its possibilities? There are two answers: mine and God's. The first is limited, in fact I might feel incompetent to deal with the situation at all, in which case the question becomes what is God going to do next? And "abandonment to the divine providence" makes much positive sense, shorn of stoicism. God's answer is unlimited, which is why providence is associated with primordial Being and must always be qualified by the adjective transcendent.

Primordial Being implies an inscrutability which does not mean that God acts as an arbitrary tyrant but that he sees infinite possibilities in a situation, most of which are hidden from us. In old-fashioned language, transcendence points to the "attributes" of omnipotence, omniscience and omnipresence.

If we think of the contrast between the very limited possibilities open to any man in a particular situation and what must be the possibilities of Being as such, we get a clue to a more intelligible and more religiously defensible meaning. God's omnipotence means that he himself, not any factical situation, is the source and also the horizon of all possibilities, and only those are excluded that are inconsistent with the structure and dynamics of God himself. "Omniscience" similarly implies freedom from a single perspective, such as is characteristic of our human knowing, for God (Being) both transcends every perspective and occupies every perspective at once. "Omnipresence" is not to be taken objectively to mean that God is diffused through space

F

like some all pervasive ether, but again that he is not tied to the factical situation that is a basic characteristic of our human "being-there".[6]

Expressive Being, incarnate in Jesus Christ, throws light on the providential situation, revealing the way of faith, commitment and sacrifice. There is no situation which cannot be illuminated by the mind of Christ as portrayed in the New Testament, which thereby becomes the key to the reading of the divine activity within providential circumstances. The mind of Christ becomes determinative of the Christian ethic, both in spirit and letter: "The awareness of the divine presence becomes the determinative factor in any distinctively Christian understanding of ethics . . . the faith that holy Being presents and manifests itself in the neighbour and even in material things lends a new depth to the world and profoundly influences behaviour in it."[7] Christian moral decision, therefore, flows from relationship with Christ, which is prayer, or the discerning of his mind in a particular situation. Bernard Häring thus sees the foundation of morality in *responsibility*, but interpreted in a startlingly literal sense: as the ability to make a response.[8] This does not rule out principle and law — or even the text-book of moral theology — but these become a codified background, a general guideline to decision. So the genuine Christian life, that is the trinitarian life, will include a meditative search for the mind of Christ in the Gospels, as well as paying due regard to the accepted principles which flow from it.

The Holy Ghost, unitive Being, is so called because he restores and maintains the unity of Being with the beings. It is he who "maketh intercession for us with groanings which cannot be uttered";[9] he is the jet-engine, the divine whirl of activity into which we sink, or float, or surrender to. "And he that searcheth the hearts knoweth what is the mind of the Spirit . . ."[10] So in the

6. *Principles of Christian Theology*, p. 189.
7. *Principles of Christian Theology*, p. 451.
8. *The Law of Christ* (Mercier, 1962), Vol. I, pp. 35–51.
9. Romans 8: 26.
10. Romans 8: 27.

concrete situation we perceive his activity as *spiritual discernment*, morally as "conscience", more widely as "prophecy", for he "spake by the prophets", and continues so to do. So the Holy Ghost is truly the spirit of unity, for he discloses the infinite possibilities of providence, inspires moral judgment based on the mind of Christ, and so directs choice.

Ideally this is a simple, spontaneous, or contemplative process, but it will be apparent that in this analysis of God's activity towards us, all the usual divisions of prayer have arisen. But they have arisen out of everyday experience, not as pious duties externally imposed.

The disclosure of Being as providential grace calls forth *praise*. In more confused situations we have spoken of *asking* about their inherent possibilities: why *has* God done this to me? What is this situation *for*? How is he challenging me? What is he up to? This is *petition* and *intercession*, according to the particular circumstances, which is a continuous, or habitual, state of life that must nevertheless be concentrated into petitionary and intercessory acts.

Strictly speaking one cannot enter into dialogue with transcendent providence, and I have certainly never suggested that Our Primordial Being who art in heaven is a proper opening for any prayer. Petition arising out of a life situation has to be focused on Christ as mediator — through Jesus Christ Our Lord — and it flows into discernment, or disclosure, which is inspired by the Holy Ghost. Starting from the practical situation it is impossible to avoid the trinitarian emphasis, so petition concludes with choice; its proper outcome is not some extraneous act or answer from God but the ability to make the correct decision, or perhaps to reinterpret the circumstances.

Trite as it may sound, the first need for serious petition is *honesty*.[11] Once we are rid of a shallow pietism we are forced to the conclusion that God acts towards us in a very peculiar way. Like the Syrophenician woman we have to argue with him,[12] not to change his mind but to discern the infinite possibilities of the situation. Like Job we must remain faithful while admitting

11. See *Christian Proficiency*, pp. 88–97.
12. Mark 7: 25–30; Matthew 15: 21–8.

bewilderment at what he can possibly be up to. The late Fr. Ray-
mond Raynes, C.R., was famous — or notorious — for his knack
of wrapping up sublime truth in apparent flippancy: "never
expect God to be helpful" he was wont to say, "work on the assumption that he will be as awkward as possible, then things run
pretty smoothly."

Fr. Raynes was expressing his sublime openness to the infinite
possibilities of providence, never expecting his plans automatically
to receive the divine rubber stamp. As acceptance of our limi-
tations is an apt description of humility — the bed-rock of
prayer — so recognition of the divine awkwardness is a homely
synthesis of the cardinal virtues of prudence and fortitude. It is
neither whining at difficult circumstances nor stoically submitting
to them, but looking for the *point*.

In similar vein, Helen Oppenheimer superbly propounds
Christ's morality as predominantly "unfair".[13] The same wage
for a gruelling day as for another's single evening hour, material
reward for thieves, passive resistance to, or rather active co-operation with, physical assault: all this cannot be rationalised or explained away. It transcends "fairness" and opens up untold
possibilities beyond it. The Father's awkwardness is matched by
the Son's unfairness; in their different ways Fr. Raynes and Helen
Oppenheimer are saying the same thing. So is St. Paul: "O the
depth of the riches both of the wisdom and knowledge of God!
How unsearchable are his judgments, and his ways past finding
out!"[14]

All this is centred on the cross of Christ, for the cross is the
supreme example of both moral unfairness — the suffering of the
just for the unjust — and the infinite possibilities of a providential
situation. And Gethsemane is the supreme example of petitionary
dialogue leading to discernment. Jesus had to argue, in bloody
sweat, before the possibilities of the cross were disclosed to him.
His obedience was not blind, his abandonment was not fatalism;
acceptance of the cross was possible only after disclosure of its
purpose.

Jesus remains active in every situation, for expressive Being is

13. *The Character of Christian Morality* (Faith Press, 1965) pp. 21–2; 66–7.
14. Romans 11:33.

agent in both creation and redemption. Therefore *meditation* on his revealed mind and ethic also springs out of the contemporary situation, for here is the key pointer to providential possibility. But Being is disclosed as both grace and judgment, and if the one leads into praise and thanksgiving the other introduces that side of the spiritual life which traditionally comes under the heading of *penitence* and *confession*. Yet once more the devotional emphases are changed and enlightened by the new map. Penitence is no longer a pious duty but a constant relation, of which confession is the concentrated act. In this sense penitence cannot be negative, rather it is the passive side of a lack of awareness of divine disclosure; it is the constructive reaction to being in a muddle over the infinity of providential possibility. Our concern is still for creative choice, not with refurbishing and patching up the stained soul-statue; consummation — "perfection" in the old language — is one with reconciliation, so the divine leading is towards more and more authentic existence, not back to the Garden of Eden.

Creation, reconciliation, and consummation, are equi-primordial, not successive, activities of God who is Trinity. Our experience of the disclosure of the Trinity has now been analysed as providence-ethics-spiritual discernment, and our response has been seen in terms of reading the providential situation, seeking the mind of Christ, and waiting on the inspiration of the Spirit. This last is the unifying principle which, ideally, knits the whole process together into a single, spontaneous knowledge of the divine will for us. This is the prayer of *contemplation*, and its creative environment is *silence*, both of which must receive more detailed treatment in due course.[15]

It must be remembered, however, that our starting point, inherent in the language of Macquarrie's reinterpretation, is a contemplative awareness of Triune Being which is forged out of daily experience. If we begin with, and continue to practise, trinitarian decision based on this analysis, then I believe that the phrase — contemplation in Triune Being — will lose some of its terror. Indeed it sounds a little frightening and "advanced" but I do not think it is all that uncommon to "ordinary" Christians.

15. *See* Chapters 12, 14 below.

Many of us do in fact ask the adventurous question: why has God done this to me? What is he up to? And without too much theo-logical speculation we spontaneously look to Jesus's sacrifice as key to an answer. All the time we realise that, although rational thought can never be excluded from responsible decision, it is not enough; we call upon the guidance of the Spirit.

I once remember having a book rejected and feeling, as it were, overjoyed with disappointment. As every writer knows the disap-pointment was real enough, and yet there was also a deep satis-fying knowledge that this was the right outcome; *right*, not only in the publisher's fair decision but right within the providential plan. I continue to thank God that that particular book never saw the light of day. And I *knew*, quite spontaneously, what I had to do next. I think most people will understand my meaning: mis-fortune, even tragedy is accepted, and that's that: but that is seldom quite so finally that. Somewhere, not least in the Gospels, there is a new glimmer of light, over the following months the Spirit gently discloses new possibilities. To the Christian such spontaneous reaction has all the marks of contemplative prayer.

Situations not only happen but develop, isolated events con-verge and make a pattern, pointing to an ongoing, providential design. This is associated with the theology of miracle,[16] not the intervention of the Father's outstretched hand but the dis-cernment of providential disclosure. Every authentic life has its "Exodus", or perhaps more than one, when a series of quite ordi-nary events converge on to an extraordinary point. God speaks, not through a transistor radio implanted in the soul-substance, not in answer to *a* prayer, not even through conscience, but in act. The whirling dynamism of Triune Being is personally disclosed. But in order to make more practical sense of this we must return to analysis and look at some practical examples.

16. *Principles of Christian Theology*, pp. 225–32.

SEVEN

The Disclosure of Being

"RELIGION is the impinging of God or Holy Being upon man's existence. The initiative is from the side of God, who gives himself to man in revelation and grace."[1] This demands the response of faith which is "acceptance and commitment in the face of Being".[2] I have discussed how Triune Being manifests himself in the situations of life as providence, sacrifice and discernment, or if you prefer, providence, morality and prophecy.

Macquarrie defines and analyses revelation as of a "gift-like character" — the divine prevenience — as

> a mood of meditation or preoccupation; the sudden in-breaking of the holy presence, often symbolised in terms of the shining of a light; a mood of self-abasement (sometimes terror, sometimes consciousness of sin, sometimes even doubt of the reality of the experience) in face of the holy; a more definite disclosure of the holy, perhaps the disclosure of a name or a purpose or a truth of some kind (this element may be called the "content" of the revelation); the sense of being called or commissioned by the holy to a definite task or way of life.[3]

He goes on to draw a distinction, if a blurred one, between revelation and "ordinary" religious experience.[4] This is clarified by William Temple's famous dictum that religious experience is the total experience of a religious man.[5] Given faith, all

1. *Principles of Christian Theology*, p. 134.
2. *Principles of Christian Theology*, p. 140.
3. *Principles of Christian Theology*, pp. 6–7.
4. *Principles of Christian Theology*, pp. 7–8.
5. *Christas Veritas* (Macmillan, 1924 ed.), pp. 37 ff.

experience is religious, but all experience is patently not revelation. Nevertheless the edges are blurred and there are types of "ordinary" experience which are more "religious" than others, and these may be qualified by such words as disclosure or in-breaking.

That we are beings let-be by Being, participating in Being, supports Temple; prayer, or our relation with God, must be a continuous process, all experience is religious. But to admit of varying degrees, types and intensity of "religiousness" in experience, is to go some way towards solving a dilemma which has worried the Church from the beginning: God is omnipresent, yet to claim experience of his presence is ever suspect; God is omnipresent but beware if this theological dogma becomes too obvious![6] The language of Being permits divine disclosure within the concrete situation to be taken seriously, but without sentimentality or suspicion. Let us look at some concrete examples.

A priest is offered a benefice and he goes to look at it. No doubt he will talk with the churchwardens, examine the accounts and registers, ascertain the stipend and so on, but if he is wise he will do much more. He will wander around it, alone, in "a mood of meditation or preoccupation", awaiting disclosure. This does not mean "praying about it" in the usual sense, or "calling on the Holy Ghost for guidance"; our priest is not listening to the transistor radio set in the middle of his soul-substance. He is "feeling" the place, as a complex of beings let-be by Being, awaiting a harmony, or rapport with it. If such a contemplative experience arises he will express it in some homely phrase like "feeling drawn to the place", or feeling that he would "be happy there". These sentiments could be superficial and self-centred, but they need not be: the integrated sense of harmony with beings and Being is the surest "answer to prayer". Needless to say this has little to do with the aesthetic or social look of the place, it could be a Cotswold village or a slum, and the manifestation of Being would most likely be concentrated in a particular being. I remember being convinced of the rightness of a job because it was a new housing estate which had retained its original hawthorn hedges. There is nothing wonderful about hawthorn hedges but on this occasion they con-

6. *See* Chapter 12 below.

stituted the particular being through which Being chose to concentrate and disclose himself. At the time I did not know of this
explanation, and reference to Father, Son and Holy Ghost offered
little help.

The contemplative disclosure may not take place, and it cannot
be forced; the point is to be able to discern it, theologically and in
the Trinity, when and if it does. The absence of such disclosure is
not decisive, although it is a pointer not to be lightly dismissed,
and one very generally accepted. "I did not warm to the job", or
"I could not see myself there" might be self-centred but it could
also be vocational ("being called or commissioned by the holy to a
definite task"). For it is a Puritan travesty of vocation to assume
that a genuine call from God must be unpleasant; true vocation,
however hard and difficult, implies some sense of satisfaction and
joy. The absence of contemplative disclosure, however, could be a
call to sacrifice, a challenge which could be expressed by "a mood
of self-abasement (sometimes terror, sometimes consciousness of
sin, sometimes even doubt of the reality of the experience) in face
of the holy". In such cases reference would switch from contemplative harmony to the mind and ethic of Christ.

But even where the contemplative decision is most real and
obvious, it would be wise to refer, or check, according to
the experienced activity of Triune Being: providence-sacrifice-
discernment. What is the providential setting of the offer of this
benefice? How did it arise, by advertisement and application
(and why not?) or by a patron's letter out-of-the-blue? If the
latter, why? What are the discernible possibilities of the job? The
answers to these questions could be decisive, events leading up to
the offer could be seen as a convergence to a disclosed point, an
"Exodus" to which, come what may and feelings notwithstanding,
there was only one answer, one proper risk. Failing any such
pattern, Christ might call to sacrifice, the morals of his mind might
make an equally sure demand, possibly unfair but promising succour. This too could be decisive, although a combination of both
is the more likely. The point is that the decision to be Christian
must be trinitarian; the complex activity of primordial, expressive
and unitive Being is the guide.

Let us take one further example before reducing the matter to

practical theology. Suppose a man and a woman wish to marry:
they are in love as the saying goes, but they are responsible people
who, boldly accepting the risk inherent in all decision, nevertheless
wish to make it as intelligently as possible, a decision in God. As
Christian people they will begin with the disclosure of the mind of
God in Christ, that is with the primordial Christian revelation
experienced as repetitive revelation: with their experience of the
mind of Christ in meditation, with Christian morals, sacrifice, succour and demand. Are there moral impediments? Has the lady
conflicting duties towards others, to dependent parents or relations? Has the man professional or vocational conflicts, in which
case where does true sacrifice lie? If these questions can be
answered satisfactorily then we are off to a good start; but
no more, and the tragedy is that this is as far as most devout
Christians go. We are off to a good start, but a very unsatisfactory
finish.

Once we take Triune Being seriously it is clear that neither
human love nor moral rules are adequate bases for a trinitarian
decision. The Church's common guidance — if so it can be
called — is that if there is no moral impediment and the couple
can take their vows seriously, then marriage is permissible. If
things go wrong, or if a genuine mistake has been made, the
couple can live the rest of their lives in misery, confident of not
having committed sin in the first place. Can we improve on
this?

The decision can be widened to embrace the implications of
providence associated with primordial Being. The initial meeting
of the man and woman, in fact any meeting between any people,
is in some sense providential. But is there here any particular,
discernible disclosure; even anything "miraculous" in the sense of
a convergence of events into a recognisably providential pattern?
Has courtship run smoothly through pre-arranged meetings, or
has there been a providential disclosure of possibilities for
sacrificial service? That "marriages are made in heaven" is profound theology by this interpretation; it only becomes trite when
God the Father is turned into a benevolent match-maker. Can
there be a genuine faith-commitment in the transcendent initiation of this proposed union? For this is an essential basis for the

stability of marriage as the Christian conceives it. Morals, love, contract and promise are all important; none is sufficient.

Providence is disclosed through both favour and judgment, God can be both helpful and transcendently awkward, Christ's ethic can be both liberating and unfair. A smooth and happy courtship is no guarantee of divine favour, neither is the principle that the course of true love never runs smoothly infallible. Although reduced to analysis we are still concerned with contemplative discernment; with life recollected in the Trinity. Acts of prayer "for the guidance of the Holy Spirit" retain their place in the scheme of things, but they are unlikely to be very successful unless, or until, they are concentrates or foci of a wider trinitarian outlook.

Have we got anywhere? If providence can be disclosed by both favour and judgment, if God can be both obviously benevolent and benevolently awkward, if love and loyalty are not enough, if everything still depends on a hoped-for disclosure; then have we not complicated things to no obvious purpose? No and Yes. No, because the trinitarian concept still makes sense of life, it still flows from existential experience: providence-sacrifice-discernment issues in a decisive synthesis which is Christian in a way that each factor taken in isolation is not. Reliance on Providence alone can be fatalism, stoicism, or possibly Deism, Sole reliance on "inspiration" is subjective and immanental, not to say Pantheistic. And the example and ethic of Christ without the other two factors is either narrowly christo-centric or legalist. These errors are likely to arise out of the very discursiveness of the Father *and* the Son *and* the Holy Ghost imagery.

But the answer to our query is Yes in so far as we have left things in an indecisive state, even if trinitarian concepts, in their fullness, have been brought into play. The need is for some supporting maps of a specialist kind, and three such guides spring to mind. The first is the principle of risk which, as the creative characteristic of God himself, is to be embraced joyfully; decision has become the positive stuff of life instead of a regrettable danger to the static purity of the soul-substance. An erroneous decision is still redeemable by the infinite possibilities of providence. But in making our choice in terms of providence-sacrifice-

discernment, we have assured that the risk involved is not that of
the gambler but of letting-be: the risk of love. The risk of letting-
be is not foolhardiness, it is co-operating with, rather than "tempt-
ing", providence.

This leads into the second specialist map which is the moral one,
and such a map *is* needed. Even in our examples of priestly vocation and human marriage, we have seen that love is not enough,
not even as a basis for risk. The activity of Triune Being therefore
condemns the extreme type of situation ethic, not because it is
existentialist or "permissive" but because it is narrowly christo-
centric rather than broadly trinitarian. It is sometimes forgotten
that the very love of Christ himself is founded on a love shared
between Father and Holy Ghost.

Macquarrie makes the point from the existential perspective:
"Like attacks on institutional religion, attacks on rules, laws, and
precepts do not sufficiently consider the embodied, historical condition of man, the relativities and ambiguities of his situation, the
differences between individuals and the need for training. Those
existentialists who deny any place to law or habit make a great
point of the *possibilities* of human existence; but they commit the
error of not recognising what the best existential analyses take into
account as equally characteristic of human existence — its *facticity*."[7]

This is why the fundamental principles of moral theology, *The
Law of Christ* as Bernard Häring calls it, remain central to trinitarian living; central, not all-embracing, and as necessary guide-
lines not as legal imperatives. But if this trinitarian approach to
life demands a moral framework, it overrules any rigorist interpretation, and gives fresh insight into the old probabilist casu-
istry. Greater or lesser probabilities can now be seen, and decided
upon, not in the negative terms of what is permissible, what one
can get away with, but according to the gloriously positive risk of
letting-be. In fact — although somewhat beyond the scope of this
book — this approach gives new meaning to many of the old
moral-theological categories: the cardinal and theological virtues,
the gifts of the Spirit, the capital sins and the "will". We have

7. *Principles of Christian Theology*, p. 462.

already noticed this with regard to faith, pride, fortitude, prudence and love; in the relation between natural ("cardinal") virtue and Christian ("theological") virtue; and in sin itself as imbalance, lostness or alienation, which is what St. Augustine meant by concupiscence.

If the problems of concrete situations are subjected to providential possibility as well as to the mind of Christ crystallised into moral doctrine, there remains the final and consummating disclosure of unitive Being: the "inspiration of the Holy Spirit". It is this inseparable connection between prayer and ethics which gives validity to choice; it is the link which renders decision Christian and trinitarian. Whether we call it the disclosure of unitive Being or the inspiration of the Spirit, we are dealing with a notoriously dangerous matter. The third specialist map we need is that which appears in spiritual theology under the heading of "Rules for the Discernment of Spirits".[8]

These old maps are wont to be drawn on an excessively large scale, mainly through an almost pathological fear of error before religious experience was brought down to earth, and before loving risk became respectable: scholastic asceticists liked to spread themselves anyway. For practical purposes five major headings can be abstracted from medieval intricacy, forming a workable scheme of reference for everyday decision.

The first is that the will of God *cannot be irrational*. Providence itself implies purpose, which may indeed be subtle, sacrificial and awkward; it may include a "miraculous" convergence of events, like the "Exodus", but in themselves they will be ordinary events. On petitionary prayer, which we have linked with the disclosure of Being, Miles Lowell Yates makes the important point that: "God is *likely to work within earth's conditions* — of course including holy words and sacraments — using them as media, ordering human life through their instrumentality, just as he creates each new human life through the medium of human parenthood. May we expect the continuance of his action towards us to be radically different from its start? And *he* has established the

8. e.g. J. de Guibert, *The Theology of the Spiritual Life*, pp. 129–36. A. Paulin, *The Graces of Interior Prayer*, pp. 638–48. R. Garrigou Lagrange, *The Three Ages of the Interior Life*, Vol. II, pp.241–8.

conditions; they mark the pattern of what he has judged needful for the development of men, if they are really to *be* men and not something else."[9] We must take account of *facticity*; we cannot choose some fantastic course of action on the grounds that the infinite providential possibility will make something of it. Jesus did not throw himself from the pinnacle of the temple because, amongst other reasons, it would have been irrational.[10] This is compatible with genuine risk, because risk is not foolhardiness; it is to be self-authenticating risk which is the risk of love, of letting-be.

The second principle is the *moral* one. If providence is actively leading in a particular situation then moral life should improve. If vocation or courtship tend to reduce temptation, and to find their expression in sacrificial love, then faith in their providential foundation is pretty secure. The basis of Christian morality is the ability to respond to Christ, which is linked with integration or harmony. This well expresses the work of unitive Being, for it means much more than the sense of well-being that an exciting job might bring, more even than the harmony betweeen lover and beloved. Morality finds its true expression only in that triune harmony within the self, with the beings, and through the beings with Being: its ultimate end is letting-be in sacrificial, risky love.

The third point flows from, and links with, the second, and is technically *abandonment*. This is manifested in the practical situation by lack of anxiety, which also spells harmony or integration, and which is classically expressed in the Sermon on the Mount.[11] If a vocational calling is characterised by fears and worries it is suspect; if one partner in courtship is distraught whenever the other makes a dangerous journey, then something is at fault. If such anxiety is lacking, or reduced to the normal bounds of frailty and facticity, then a mature faith in providential disclosure is upheld. In old-fashioned language it is abandonment, in the new language it is acceptance of the risk of letting be.

Fourthly, a true discernment of spirits involves a *flexibility of purpose*. A decision about a providential leading, or concerning

9. *God in Us* (S.P.C.K. 1960), p. 159.
10. *Principles of Christian Theology*, p. 263.
11. Matthew 6: 25–34.

the inspiration of the Holy Ghost, is suspect if its outcome is too narrowly assumed or planned, for this is a failure to accept the infinite possibilities of transcendent providence. The will of God, within the practical situation, is unlikely to be discerned as a rigidly predetermined plan, but rather as a leading into more expansive possibilities of being. Vocation to the priesthood, or to anything else, ought to embrace considerations as to the man's abilities, gifts, enthusiasms and failings, but it is unwise to map a career too precisely. The leading of God implies flexibility of purpose, for God himself is concerned with human choices and potentialities, not with polishing up the soul-substance statue and re-erecting it in Eden.

The fifth point is something of a synthesis of the other four and has constantly cropped up during their discussion: it is that *integration* or *harmony* which arises out of the interpretation of life in terms of Triune Being. Our whole analysis of choice, decision, interpretation in terms of the Trinity's activity, is but a background, a second-best, to that spontaneity of discernment which springs from the recollected, or integrated life. The core of Christian living in its fullness is an habitual awareness of Being, a constant but unforced anticipation of the divine disclosure. This is in accord with tradition — the good tree brings forth good fruit without arguing — (or theologising) about it. Where we break with tradition is in its assumption that such religious experience is extremely rare and reserved to particularly advanced and holy people. The classic writers are correct in regard to the type of experience they describe — that on the mystical-theological level — but they refuse to acknowledge that there is genuinely contemplative experience on a much more common and homely level.[12]

An analogy of such experience is that of a writer searching for exactly the correct word to express a thought. He may seek discursively, resorting to dictionary and thesaurus, but usually to no avail: suddenly the word "springs to mind", and he *knows* that it is the right one. The same process occurs in the solution of a crossword puzzle; after much pondering and searching the right

12. *See* Chapter 12 below.

word presents itself. There is no need to count up the letters to see if it fits, you *know* that it does. Such everyday experience bears all the marks of contemplation; it concerns the whole integrated being, the sensitive eyes, the intellect, and a deeper intuition. It is a synthetic, momentary, spontaneous disclosure in which the man, the word, the puzzle all add up to a harmony, everything fits.

A similar, yet even more common experience arises out of familiar things and places. It is the harmonious confluence of things and loved ones — beings — which make for "at-home-ness". Here the beings may well disclose Being. Or the cricketer on his home ground: bat-on-ball, linseed oil, tea on the terrace and beer on the balcony. So with the golfer in his club, the artist in his studio, the traveller in his native town. All this is "natural" contemplation, and if we start with Temple's religious man then it is akin to contemplative prayer: the occasion to seek God — and to choose in the Trinity.

It is still a question of language, and my quarrel with the classicists — if such it is — and my disquiet with the ancient formulae, is that they do not begin at the beginning; they do not start low enough and are loath to accept the lowly as genuine. Father, Son and Holy Ghost contain greater riches than the language of Being, yet they seem very remote from crosswords, golfclubs and cricket bats. If we start with Being actively letting-be the beings, then Temple's dictum makes a special sort of sense; the daily situation opens up trinitarian depths.

When the classical tradition does deign to permit the manifestation of God through the contemplation of things, then, following the substantive formulae, those things are invariably static: the crucifix, statuette and pious symbol. New-map language points rather to the active situation; not only the mystical light and the mystical night but the physical haze and the physical fog could be genuine manifestations of Being. Traditional prayers for rain and fine weather have become an embarrassment, because it is almost impossible to avoid the symbol of God sitting on his cloud with a solar torch in one hand and a watering-can in the other, dispensing favour and judgment according to whim. Yet it is the situation, including roaring east winds, hailstorms, and cloud formations, that truly discloses the activity of Being; not because the static Trinity is playing games with the elements or painting pictures in the sky, but because all the beings disclose Being anyway and all the time. It is the language of Being that changes the *Benedicite* from a pious nursery-rhyme into the most tremendous theology, ultimately opening up a deeper understanding of Father, Son and Spirit.

EIGHT

Jesus Christ: Human-Being

IN SPITE of my prefatory apology about the difficulty of arranging this book, the reader may be wondering what has happened to all the people. Cherry trees, golfclubs and hailstorms are all very well but is not the essence of Christianity, and of prayer, commitment to the Person of Christ? Is not the central expression of Christian life love of one's neighbour? The primordial revelation is a Person not a creed or a book: have I not taken a long time to get around to people? If human being is always being-with-others, and if existence involves community, then this criticism is especially pertinent, and no doubt the book could have been arranged differently. Nevertheless I think there is something to be said for the course I have followed.

We must have some idea of God before we can speak meaningfully about his incarnation, that is why we need the Old Testament, and although Christ unveils God's Fatherhood and sends the Holy Spirit, we have seen that the trinitarian concept is inherent in human experience. Being is first disclosed through things, then more fully through human existents, and finally in Christ, the supreme human-Being. This is the fundamental progression of spiritual awakening: creatures-existents-Being. Dr. Mascall puts it very well:

Man, then, is a social being, and lives in a social context. Nevertheless it is a sheer mistake to suppose that his relationships are purely social ones and that he can fulfil himself by attending exclusively to the latter. By the very fact that he has a body, he is part of the world of nature as well as of the world of persons. ... No philosophy of human life can be adequate if it concentrates simply on the relationship in which the individual stands to other human individuals and ignores that in which he stands to the entire universe.[1]

Nevertheless:

We have seen that Being is present and potentially manifest in all beings, but that since these constitute a hierarchy, some are capable of manifesting Being in a greater range than others. The highest place in this hierarchy was claimed for personal beings. Now among these personal beings a special claim is being made for Jesus Christ, as the person in whom Being has been signally present and manifest, that is to say, has achieved its advent and epiphany.[2]

What, then, does the incarnation mean in the practice of prayer, seen primarily as relation? What does it mean to personal relationships and to community? How does it tie up with intercession? How does it fully disclose Being? The question turns on christology, which translates these questions into very practical theology: How does one "meet Christ", and enter into dialogue with him? What does it mean to be "in Christ"? And what is meant by the fashionable idea of "seeing Christ in others"?

The original map says very little; simply that Jesus Christ was conceived by the Holy Ghost and born of the Virgin Mary. He is therefore Son of God and son of woman: God-man. The *Quicunque Vult* elaborates, pointing to the official large-scale map known to the Church as the Definition of Chalcedon.[3] Here Christ is the incarnate Son of God, fully human and fully divine, two natures in one person, the humanity and the divinity never to be either separated or confused. This formula has been subjected to argument for fifteen hundred years, and we are back with a vengeance amongst the little yellow humps in Eggardon Hundred: "persons", "natures", "substance" and all the rest. From this God-manhood issues that pile of rough charts — one can

1. *The Christian Universe* (Darton, 1966), pp. 90–91.
2. *Principles of Christian Theology*, p. 270.
3. *Principles of Christian Theology*, p. 273.

hardly speak of a map — which comprise the Church's speculations upon the manner of the atonement.

St. Bernard attempted to re-draw this map for the special purpose of devotion, and from here springs the traditional method of
meeting Christ in meditative prayer. We know by faith that the
risen and glorified Christ is somehow "present", yet, as it were,
invisible to the physical eye. He is made present through the imagination, and through reflection upon his words and works as
given in the Gospels, concluding with some resolution or, with
luck, some fresh insight into his mind. This kind of devotion, based
on the discursive statements of Chalcedon, has served Christians
tolerably well for centuries. Today it is suspect, if not wholly discredited, for it seems artificial and remotely pious. It also presents
considerable theological difficulties, for it is based on an image of
Christ involving physical characteristics about which no word can
be found in the New Testament. We are also back on the theological tightrope: here is the person of Jesus, which embraces two
separate natures, but no, they are not separate; but yes they are,
although not to be separated. One enters into dialogue — petition
and intercession — with Christ in his humanity, and through it to
God. But who are you really talking to? Christ's divine nature or
God the Father, or both, or the Trinity? Perhaps after all we can
do without any symbolic image of the man Jesus? But no we
cannot, for commitment is not to commands and precepts but to a
person, and if Christ's human nature is real it must be clothed with
flesh **and blood.**

If this kind of prayer is discredited there is another way of
approach, as old as St. Paul yet enjoying a current vogue, as
popular in its appeal as it is unformulated in theology. Christ's
human nature is something in which we somehow share; I am "in
Christ" and he dwells in me: "I live; yet not I, but Christ liveth in
me."[4] Christ the second Adam recapitulates all humanity within
himself, so he dwells in all people — for simplicity's sake let us say
that he dwells in a particular friend, Henry. I can now approach
Christ, converse with Christ, love and serve him, not through some
shady devotional image but in Henry. Christ in others: that is the

4. Galatians 2: 20.

modern plea. But if we stick to Chalcedon we still confront im-
mense christological difficulties. It must be insisted, for example,
that it is truly Christ who dwells in Henry, not some vagary like
the Christian spirit, or the love of Jesus. It must be equally
strongly insisted that Henry remains Henry, he is not swallowed
up in the sacred humanity. The same applies to me, so when I
speak with Henry there is a remarkable double-dialogue between
four — or is it six? — "natures": Henry's, mine, Christ's humanity
and Christ's divinity. The ramifications of such colloquy (who is
talking to whom?) need not be elaborated. Further, what exactly
is meant by the "sacred humanity", or the human "nature" of
Christ which is a recapitulation of all humanity? Is this just
another name for humanity at large, which is in some vague sense
"sacred"? Or does it refer to a kind of foggy "universal", some all-
pervading substance, into which we are incorporated? Conversely
is the sacred humanity itself a substance injected or "infused" into
other static soul-substances?

This is another parody of the practical situation; the faithful
generally manage to steer their way through such theological intri-
cacy, usually by being happily unaware of it. But if the plea for a
spirituality based on the love and service of Christ in others is to be
taken seriously, as I think it deserves to be, these difficulties cannot
be evaded. The old question arises: venerable and accurate as the
Chalcedonian map undoubtedly is, natures, substances, and similar humps in Eggardon Hundred, might we not get on better with
a new one?

I return to my premise, the value of a map is demonstrated by
its use, so I set out on my journey not with metaphysical theories
about Christ's natures but with my experience of Henry. I live in
this world, a being-with-others, a being-with-Henry, and I believe
in the creed, which here speaks of God incarnate.

In my primary experience, however, God is not Christ but
Triune Being whom Christ manifests. Primordial Being moves out
through expressive Being to let-be all the beings — including me
and Henry. Unitive Being strives constantly, actively, in a whirl of
power, with groanings that cannot be uttered, to unite us more
perfectly with Being and with one another. We both participate
in, and manifest Being, so we have a common relationship in

Christ without bothering about recapitulated substances or infused natures. It is, indeed, to say that we are adopted sons of God and brothers in Christ but to me at any rate that does not drive home in quite the same way, it is too theoretical and too vaguely sentimental.

The next thing I notice about my experience of Henry is that he has no fixed "nature", no fixed stock of characteristics, but rather an existence, potentiality, becoming, a being-alive-ness, which distinguishes him from other existents. Henry is an "emerging", a coming-to-light: he exists. This is no academic theory but common-sense experience, for when I think of Henry I am immediately aware of his physical appearance, but this is not Henry and when I describe him I seldom bother to mention his height, weight and hair colour. I say that he is kind, generous and loyal, but these are not fixed characteristics, little bits of substance implanted into his static soul. They rather describe the way he usually acts, and to accept Henry is an act of faith because he might on occasion behave uncharacteristically. He might act unkindly towards me, he might betray me, he is not kind and loyal in the same way as an orange is round.

So Henry is not as a little human hut in which Christ dwells: the "soul" as "temple of the Holy Ghost" is another classic symbol which can bear a valid interpretation, but it is very misleading as it stands.

The next step is the crux of the matter: if Henry has no fixed "nature" then neither has Christ; the "sacred humanity" becomes the supreme manifestation of existence. To describe Jesus as fully human, or "perfect man", means that he exhibits existence at its most authentic.[5] Existence is potentiality, an emerging or coming-to-light; it is "open-ended".[6] Christ is divine since he is the incarnation of expressive Being and

It is through expressive Being that God emerges from his hiddenness and comes to light. But clearly this self-manifestation of Being can take place most fully in a particular being that has no fixed "nature" but whose very "nature" is an existence, an

5. *Principles of Christian Theology*, pp. 270–76.
6. *Principles of Christian Theology*, pp. 273.

emerging, so that it can express more and more Being. If we can think of expressive Being (the Logos) finding perfect expression in a particular being (and such a being could only be a personal or existent being), then in this particular being the two natures would come together in a unity.[7]

"God really does in a manner put himself into what he creates, in varying degrees."[8] Being is present and manifest in all the beings, but the incarnation means that Christ, the second person of the Trinity, puts himself fully and completely into an existent being. This is the ultimate of theism, Christ is focus of Being, "christhood is the goal towards which created existence moves".[9]

This type of christology begins, as Macquarrie puts it, "from below up, from the human career that is received as the revelation of God, rather than from the notion of the pre-existent Logos that has then to be conceived as taking a body and appearing as a particular existent".[10] It is surprising that this process should be so feared by the faithful. So long as we think in Chalcedonian terms we risk a split between the two natures — the Nestorian heresy — and from below up is clearly the New Testament pattern: "To the first Christian disciples and to their successors, Jesus of Nazareth appeared as the revelation of the Father; he was, so to speak, seen in depth as the particular being in whom the presence and manifestation of Being itself has been focused. Yet this same Jesus could be seen also as just another member of the human race, as indeed he was . . ."[11]

The disciples knew that Jesus was man long before they realised that he was God, and as the quotation points out, so did their successors. In spite of metaphysical christology, St. Bernard's far-reaching contribution to prayer was precisely this beginning from below up, in fact from "carnal love".[12] So with the mainstream of medieval devotion, Christ is approached through his humanity

7. *Principles of Christian Theology*, p. 275.
8. *Principles of Christian Theology*, p. 275.
9. *Principles of Christian Theology*, p. 276.
10. *Principles of Christian Theology*, p. 252.
11. *Principles of Christian Theology*, p. 251.
12. *De Diligendo Deo*, the first degree of love.

which becomes, as it were, the gateway to God. When this is placed within the context of the Church — the Body of Christ — the medievals, especially in the fourteenth century, began with the sacred humanity manifested in the faithful: in fact in Henry. This is existential common-sense, for it is meaningless to speak of Christ's humanity without reference to the humanity we know in the world.

Christ is in others in varying degrees, he emerges as people move towards christhood, which makes a good deal of sense of the so-called "cult of the saints". But Henry is no saint, yet I see Christ in him as expressive Being actively at work. Henry, like St. Paul, has not already attained, he presses on towards the goal, he is on the way. Henry is no longer a human temple, solidly stuck, in which two or three "natures" sit in a static group, but an emerging towards christhood. To see Christ in Henry means to watch his potentialities develop, to see him attain to fuller existence, to manifest more and more being, and this is to see Christ at work in his triple activity of creation, reconciliation and consummation. The end product is to see and respond to Henry's growing ability to love, or let-be.

All this process happens to me as well, however gradually and grudgingly, I move towards christhood, towards a larger capacity for letting-be. I am not only to see Christ in Henry but to serve Henry in Christ: to see and to serve means to praise and to love. In this sense my relation with Christ in Henry may be called prayer, the end product of which is a sharing of the scared humanity in love: prayer and ethics are indissociable.

Everybody knows that the word *love* takes first prize for ambiguity, and that it serves to translate at least three Greek words of subtly different meanings; *agape* — love in Christ; *philia* — human friendship; and *eros* — carnal or sensual love. Although these meanings and differences are important, I must now boldly suggest that, within the incarnational context, the verb *to let-be* becomes a simplification which comprehends them all. If I truly see Christ in Henry — to avoid confusion let us here speak of Henrietta — and if we share in the sacred humanity existentially, with our total, integrated beings, then these subtle distinctions become superfluous.

I have quoted from William Temple that religious experience is the total experience of a religious man, and we have seen that this makes especially good sense when religion is understood as awareness of Being manifested in the beings; more particularly when prayer is seen primarily as continuous relation with God. Temple is also associated with another well known aphorism, although I suspect that it is not original to him: that Christianity is the most materialistic of all religions. From the pulpit this is received with devout approval: yes, God created all things very good; colour, music, flowers and pictures all lead into a wider sacramentalism; food and drink are to be received with thanksgiving and enjoyed in moderation, and so on. But it remains a substantive statement, a cold academic fact. Translated into terms of existential dynamic the idea becomes very startling indeed, for in terms of human activity and experience materialism becomes sensuality: Christianity is the most sensuous of all religions.

I use the word in its literal sense, pertaining to sensory experience, not in its prostituted form which implies voluptuousness. If we put both of Temple's sayings together, in the context of Being who participates in and is manifested in the beings, then the sharing of sensory experience with Henry — or Henrietta — is a true participation in the sacred humanity. If I give Henry "a cup of cold water only in the name of a disciple"[13] then I am not just performing a kind action, for "inasmuch as ye have done it unto one of the least of these my brethren, ye have done it unto me".[14] I am seeing and serving Christ, expressive Being is manifestly active. If Henry relishes the cold water to slake a burning thirst — a wonderfully sensuous experience — and if he shares it with me in like condition, then our experience of Christ is more not less. If we managed to rustle up a couple of dry martinis the experience could be more religious still.

D. H. Lawrence is famous — or notorious — for the suggestion that sexual intercourse is an act of Holy Communion: why stick at that? No doubt he chose this particular example for its emotive and provocative impact, but the taste of coffee, the smile of a child, the embrace of lovers, the smell of a cherry tree, the sound of

13. Mark 9: 41; Matthew 10: 42.
14. Matthew 25: 40.

music, or any other such experience can be holy communion: that is a manifestation of expressive Being incarnate, a sharing in the sacred humanity.

This is nonsense if we lose sight of the essential premise: the *total* experience of a *religious man*. And a religious man in our sense is one who interprets his life in terms of the Trinity, who is aware of the disclosure of Being in the beings, who commits himself to Christ in a continuing prayer-relation.

It is also nonsense if we lose sight of the fact that the practical end-product of the movement towards christhood is the ability to let-be. If we stretch the word love — and it is almost infinitely stretchable — it might be made to cover indulging a spoilt child, getting drunk with a friend or sexual promiscuity, but these things cannot possibly be qualified as letting-be.

It is in this fully incarnational sense that the distinctions between *agape, philia* and *eros* become blurred, for I am concerned with total human experience — existence or being-aliveness — which is shared between Christian and Christ. *Philia* — friendship — between me and Henry, *eros* between me and Henrietta, both take on elements of *agape* once Christ is truly seen and experienced in others. It seems a little curious that in traditional devotion all this is quite acceptable in terms of sensory pain but not when it concerns pleasure. The sick have always been exhorted to link their physical sufferings with those of the Passion and the Cross, even the subtler pain of being mocked, spurned and humiliated has its devotional counterpart in the Passion. Is there serious christological reason why the enjoyment of good wine should not constitute a similar sharing in the sacred humanity at the Cana wedding feast? It is the whole of experience which must move towards christhood: that is the ultimate recapitulation.

NINE

Community of Faith

FOLLOWING THE traditional pattern, *Christian Proficiency* began with the doctrine of the Church, as the necessary environment of prayer. The present study could have started in the same way because membership of the Church is part of my present experience. Macquarrie has also insisted that theological speculation is impossible except from within the community of faith.

In another sense, however, consideration of the doctrine of the Church properly belongs to the end rather than to the beginning of the section of the present book. "Most basic of all the characteristics of religion is the impinging of God or Holy Being upon man's existence. The initiative is from the side of God, who gives himself to man in revelation and grace."[1] This is the ancient doctrine of divine prevenience: God must convert, or at least initiate the conversion process, before membership of the Church is sought. The Church is the Body of Christ and belief in God precedes faith in his incarnation. I do not know what influence the local church had on my childhood. I remember nothing about it but I remember the cherry tree as if it were yesterday. The beings disclosing Being, existents manifesting more Being, then the nurture of this experience within the community of faith: this seems the natural order of things.

Eventually the Church becomes necessary to me. That will sound self-centred and impious to those whose piety turns upon such phrases as "Holy Mother Church", but it is the more realistic way round. The Church becomes necessary to be because man is social and faith must be shared, or as I should prefer to put it, existence is always being-with-others. "The expression 'self' should not mislead us into thinking of the solitary individual, for

1. *Principles of Christian Theology*, p. 134.

authentic selfhood is possible only in a community of selves, and we have seen already that among the polarities to be held in tension are community and individuality."[2] The experience of Being disclosed in life also has to be concentrated into acts of prayer, otherwise prayer-as-relation degenerates into theory. Such concentrated acts may begin personally, but their corporate counterpart soon becomes necessary. In my better moments the awesome disclosure of Holy Being initiates spontaneous praise. Still in my better moods such spontaneity is sometimes lacking, yet the deep desire to praise remains. This creates frustration which is overcome by the habit of disciplined corporate acts. There are many degrees and variations of these my better moods, until I reach my worst moods, which, regrettably, are much more frequent. These are periods of dullness and apathy in which Being remains hidden, periods of disharmony and alienation which ultimately lead into penitence. There are situations when the providential awkwardness of the Father and the unfairness of the Son's demands are not easily accepted. Frailty and sin necessitate a discipline which must have its corporate aspect, for I need the support of faithful friends.

Choice is the stuff of life, decision creates selfhood, and although choice and decision must be my own, this does not preclude support and guidance. I need the supporting friendship and corporate wisdom of the community of faith, and I may need counsel, spiritual guidance, and pastoral-theological interpretation of my particular situation. In the Preface I argued that every pastor, and ultimately every serious Christian, must make his own theological adaptation to meet every unique situation: you cannot write pastoral-theology like a cook-book. It is rather handed down, stage by stage, from scholar to others. I may need help in this process, not to make my decisions for me but in order that I may make them more effectively.

If this is how the need for the Church arises out of experience it in no way dictates a theology of the Church; it does not mean that I wish to create my own Church or to bring the existing one round to my own way of thinking. The Church is part of my -ontological

2. *Principles of Christian Theology*, p. 64.

premise, part of the given, and part of the creed I put my faith in.
But starting this way round does influence my way of approach to
the community of faith, and it will not be surprising that this is best
expressed and understood with reference to the ancient doctrine of
the Church reinterpreted by new-map language.

Let us begin by asserting that the Church is already implicit in
creation. We have seen that creation is the self-outpouring of
Being, whereby there is getting built up a commonwealth of
beings freely united in love. The Church is a necessary stage in
this great action of Being, so that to believe in creation is
already to believe in the Church, and there is a sense in which
the Church was there "in the beginning" and is co-eval with the
world.[3]

The Church is a stage in the process that leads from creation
through reconciliation to consummation. The end of this movement is the kingdom of God, an all-embracing commonwealth
of love and freedom, in which all humanity — and indeed all
creation — will be renovated and transformed.[4]

This leads into the Body of Christ doctrine, for expressive Being
is agent in both creation and reconciliation. Expressive Being is
the Logos that became incarnate in Jesus Christ, so there is a sense
in which his "Body" must be co-eval with creation. We have also a
language pattern which completely rules out all the errors which,
in one way or another, cast doubt upon the complete divinity of
the incarnate Son.

The incarnation was explicated in terms of the coming together
of the human and the divine, of a creaturely being with Being,
or again, in terms of the raising of manhood to God-manhood.
The Church is to be understood as the community in which this
raising of manhood to God-manhood, which we see in Christ,
continues. The Church therefore is rightly called the "body of

3. *Principles of Christian Theology*, p. 347.
4. *Principles of Christian Theology*, pp. 391–2.

Christ" which is its most appropriate title . . . the Church is an
on-going incarnation.[5]

The Church has here undergone the same transformation as
beings and existents. It is no longer "grounded" in the sacred
humanity understood as Christ's human "nature", for neither
Christ nor anyone else has a "nature" in this sense of a fixed stock
of characteristics attached to a soul-substance. The Church has
ceased to be a stable, rooted thing and has sprung to life. It is
concerned not so much with maintaining itself in an ecclesiastical
status quo but with on-going mission and ultimate death; its
marks are not stability but fluidity, not safety but creative risk. As
the self is not a statue to be repaired, cleaned and polished, but a
potentiality to be fulfilled, so the Church is no ark of salvation to
be patched up and kept afloat but a potentiality to be achieved.
This is perfectly in keeping with the mainstream of traditional
doctrine, although it shatters some devotional ideas which have
crept in. The Church is no longer a pompous and autocratic
matriarch but it is the body of Christ; it is no ark of salvation but it
is an extension of the incarnation; it is no shelter for the faithful
but it is the community of faith.

How does, or how can, this sort of Church serve those needs
which have arisen out of experience? The first such need was for
community, for being-with-others, and we must try to define this
vague and fashionable word.

A rich diversity is undoubtedly a source of great strength to the
Christian community as a whole. Yet it is clear that everything
cannot be left to a particular situation or its context. A community requires an identity. The stronger a community is, the
richer diversity it can contain, yet there is a critical point somewhere when the diversity begins to subvert the identity of the
community and begins its dissolution. There have to be some
identifying characteristics of the community, running through
all its diversity.[6]

The dilemma is as old as I Corinthians 12, and as usual the

5. *Principles of Christian Theology*, p. 348.
6. *Principles of Christian Theology*, pp. 338–9.

pendulum has swung from one side to the other throughout history. Sometimes the Church has been so rigidly corporate and autocratic that individuality has been well nigh crushed; sometimes — and the modern English parish is a fair example — individuality is so stressed that community is apt to disintegrate.

The modern situation, and the prayer and life which has evolved from within it, tends towards the latter end of the scale, for although the community emphasis is popular, existentialism gives particular value to choice, decision, and personal authenticity. What then, are the identifying characteristics of the modern Church which will subserve the needs for community?

It could be argued that the stress we have placed on creation, and on prayer as relation concentrated into acts, supports traditional parochialism as creative of community; community arises from people living together. It could be argued further that if prayer is experience concentrated into corporate acts, and especially the eucharist, then it is logical to concentrate creation itself into a focal setting in which these acts took place. In this sense a concentrate of place and a consecrated place become much the same thing. But modern mobility, as well as the current stress on individualism, frustrates this venerable pattern. Moreover, the traditional stress on corporate stability, implied in both monasticism and the Book of Common Prayer, presupposes a theology of the Church which is no longer tenable. For the Church can no longer be understood as a static foundation, rooted in Christ's substantial human "nature"; it is an on-going incarnation, an emergence, a fluid open-ended structure. Geographical boundaries, in themselves, no longer create community, and although the eucharist remains the central bond of Christian unity, the local congregation has ceased to exhibit identifying characteristics. And no amount of artificially constructed parochial plans can alter this situation.

Most of the other traditional marks of the Christian community come under the same condemnation; belief in the creeds, acceptance of the Bible, baptism, even commitment to Jesus, are both too vague and too substantive as hallmarks of the modern community of faith, although indeed they all still apply to it. The identifying characteristic for which we seek must be prayer, but since prayer is central to all religion it must be prayer of a specifically Christian kind. The eucharist is certainly this, yet we have seen that the contemporary congregation, however eucharistically centred, does not necessarily or automatically achieve community. The answer arising out of our study of experience and its needs is for this prayer — *common* prayer — to be both trinitarian and a concentrate of an awareness of the disclosure of Being expressed as praise. The first evolves as experience of Being in life becomes more and more trinitarian in terms of both prayer-acts and supra-moral decision. Ultimately it is the general, contemplative trinitarian interpretation of life that forges unity between Christians and so creates community.

The second factor — the common concentrate of praise — is traditionally supplied by the divine office. But it has been shown that, although something like the office has arisen as a need growing out of experience, it is unsatisfactory in most of its present forms. And it is unsatisfactory in both theory and practice; in theory because it is grounded in a static Church theology, assuming a geographic stability of population, and in practice because few modern Christians are attracted to this complex form of prayer, and do not use it. Our answer is to return to a pre-Prayer Book and pre-monastic age; to the primitive Church which is our accepted pattern.

Did the disciples, a close-knit body of friends in the constant company of Jesus himself, need or desire any such bond of common prayer? On the surface it looks unlikely, yet Joachim Jeremias translates Luke 11: 1, not as "Lord, teach us to pray . . ." but "Lord, teach us a prayer . . ." The implication behind the disciple's request is for some formula as a bond of unity between them; a kind of signature tune, national anthem, or regimental march. This was to be "a distinguishing formula to be used either in addition to the traditional prayers or actually as a substitute for them. At any rate, as we shall see shortly, the Church regarded the Lord's Prayer as a substitute for the three daily Jewish prayers long before the gospels were composed."[7] By this criterion a good

7. *The Prayers of Jesus* (S.C.M. 1967), **p.** 77.

case can be made for regarding the Lord's Prayer itself as the original Christian "office". The point will be of importance later.

Experience has also dictated a need for community as support and guidance. The liturgy and common prayer lend spiritual support to the individual Christian, but these do not necessarily provide personal guidance. In pastoral practice there must always be a middle term — the Church local — between the individual and the Church universal, and it is notorious that the parochial congregation fails to supply this need. It is supplied, however, by something smaller and more spontaneous: the family, house-church, cell, or natural group of friends. For guidance, like prayer itself, becomes a continuous relational stimulus rather than a series of formal acts or interviews.

The specific functions of the priesthood remain[8] but these too are transformed in the light of our new interpretation. Guidance may still be forthcoming from this professional quarter, but it will be the guidance of a pastoral-theologian rather than that of a clerical autocrat. Choice may be guided but it has to be one's own; decision depends upon a trinitarian interpretation of a situation in which, guidance notwithstanding, the personal risk of letting-be largely overrules, or at least mitigates the virtue of obedience. It is not surprising that, from the influence of modern culture as well as of theology, the large "institutional" congregation, and clericalism, are in decline.

Having begun from this existential standpoint, even from the blatantly personal, we may now pass to a more objective consideration of the Church's mission; we move from my experienced need for the Church to my service of others from within it. First of all we echo *Christian Proficiency* in asserting a vicarious quality to the Church's prayer: one can pray *for* in two senses, the straight intercessory for, but also for-on-behalf-of, or instead-of. This is inherent in any theology of the Body of Christ, for the life of Christ was one of unbroken prayer-relation with the Father and his redemptive sacrifice was *for* the whole world. An extension of the incarnation, the work of the Body of Christ must follow this

8. *Principles of Christian Theology*, pp. 388–91.

H

vicarious pattern. But *Christian Proficiency* — with due regard for the inherent dangers — extended the metaphor suggesting that eucharist and prayer might be seen as pulse and heartbeat of the Body. This in turn assumed a Church grounded in Christ's human "nature", which, if kept in health, would automatically grow. I even resorted to the analogy in which the Church was a machine, prayer keeping it oiled, polished, and in working order. Shades of the statue-image, for by implication it was a stationary engine which did not go anywhere: perhaps the same devotional thought arises when the parish church is spoken of as the "powerhouse of the parish".

Admittedly this is rather strained. Nevertheless, by the new interpretation these analogies make more sense than they did before. If prayer begins in the world of beings, if the total life of religious men is religious experience, if the Church is inherent in creation, an on-going incarnation, a movement from manhood to christhood, then prayer as pulse and heartbeat takes on more real and dynamic implications. The stationary engine turns into a roaring locomotive, and prayer makes the wheels go round.

Prayer is vicarious, the leaven in the lump and the salt in the stew, but it is also springboard to action, to service in and to the world. "The ministry of the Church is quite simply and ade-quately described by St. Paul as 'the ministry of reconciliation' . . . The ministry of reconciliation is the ministry of responding to those in need, and without this, any other kind of ministry is empty. This fundamental ministry is our co-operation in God's great work of letting-be."[9] Response to those in need is to be understood in its widest sense, and charitable works, however humble, are never to be despised, for these are Henry's cups of cold water truly manifesting the sacred humanity. We must be warned, however, that charity in its prostituted sense, or even love in its sentimental sense, and possibly evangelism in some of its senses, can produce the exact opposite of letting-be.

The universal need, the fundamental mission of the Church, is that fullness of letting-be, enabling to be or empowering to exist more authentically, which comes about through reconciliation. In

9. *Principles of Christian Theology*, pp. 374, 376.

its primary sense this means the restoration of harmony, the re-
dressing of alienation and imbalance, within the self, with the created environment, with others in society, and with God: in
existence, with the beings, existents, and Being. In terms of
spiritual theology this letting-be comes under two inter-related
headings: contemplation and forgiveness.

Contemplative prayer is the opposite of disharmony or imbalance. So we have a link between prayer, life and service that
was far less obvious on the old map. There prayer and confession
were factors which could be related to practical problems, but the
links of relevance had to be fitted together. The root of our practical problems is now seen to be the opposite of contemplation,
the development of which is not merely relevant for it *is* the solution. Existence grows with decision, so choice in Triune
Being — providence-sacrifice-discernment — is as practical an
issue as can be imagined. Acts of prayer are foci of the total
process: life and prayer are one. This does not claim to make
things easy, still less comfortable; there is still God's providential
awkwardness and Christ's unfairness, with sacrifice in the middle.
Nevertheless we have a framework within which all problems are
either solved or interpreted; made sense of.

Reconciliation also means confession and forgiveness. There is
nothing to add to the theology of Penance except to note further
clarification when this is placed on the new map. There is no
essential conflict between sacramental and "private" confession;
most serious Christians resort to both methods. This *via media*
position makes even more sense when penitence is seen to be alienation or lostness in daily experience, concentrated in the act of
confession. Recollective, "private", and sacramental confession
now become one integrated movement towards Being instead of
three legitimate but isolated acts. Moreover, if sin strains the relation, or even separates man from God, restoration and reconciliation with the Father, Son and Holy Ghost offers considerable
devotional difficulties: are we acquitted by the almighty Judge?
Are we back in the arms of Christ after a lover's tiff? Has the
incarnate Son turned his back on us only to turn round beaming
benevolence after absolution? Another parody no doubt, but it is
difficult to avoid some such devotional symbol on the old map. On

a more theological plane, being restored to a "state of grace" has been a notorious difficulty since the doctrine was first mooted. Even Aquinas was stretched to the full to find his way through its maze of intricacy, so here is hardly a doctrine, however valid in itself, to commend to ordinary Christians in their search for simplicity. The sinking back into harmony with Being, devotionally elaborated into Father and incarnate Son if need be, is more satisfactory.

A further old-map difficulty is that, while absolution must be regarded as an inviolable and effective sacramental act, through which reconciliation and forgiveness are absolutely complete, it does not eradicate our weaknesses neither are the results of sin entirely done away. The old manuals speak of "washing away" the sin which nevertheless leaves "a stain on the soul". We have seen the weakness inherent in this kind of substantive image, the polishing of the soul-statue idea. The old manuals are here in difficulty, yet they do speak to common experience. A Christian murderer can truly accept absolution but it is far-fetched to assume that he can completely forget that he has killed a man; that the sin is washed away as if it had not been. This is the existential truth theology tries to uphold. Things are simplified, and nothing is lost, by re-thinking in terms of full restoration into the harmony of Triune Being while past sins become part of the factical situation to be *accepted*. We are made by our decisions, including the decision to commit sin. Our sinfulness, though not to be confused with facticity,[10] becomes part of our present existence. This is more satisfactory than breaking and restoring friendly relations with God despite "stains on the soul". Finitude and facticity mean uncertainty, genuine existence involves risk; forgiveness of sin as passport to safety is about as unChristian a thing as can be imagined.

There is one further difficulty which necessitates my crossing a friendly sword with Dr. Macquarrie. The Church is an emergence, a coming-to-light, an on-going incarnation, which is inherent in creation itself and so there can be no hard and fast distinction between it and the world. "The Church is for all men, for what goes on in the Church, as we have seen, is simply the

10. *Principles of Christian Theology*, pp. 44–5, 210–11, 243.

spearhead of what is going on in the creation as a whole. The end of the Church and the end of creation converge upon the kingdom of God. The Church cannot be complete until the whole creation is complete, and then of course the distinction between the Church and the rest of creation will have disappeared."[11]

If that refutes the ark of salvation idea, if it takes creation seriously and implies that the grace of God is wider than the Church of Christ, then nobody today is likely to quarrel with it. But can you speak of a "spearhead" with blurred and blunted edges? And, whatever the difficulties of pressing the Body of Christ analogy, can any sort of body be incomplete? The infant body is immature, it could be diseased, undeveloped, embryonic, a potential, but can it be incomplete?

Macquarrie says some harsh and laudable things against an arrogant, over-zealous proselytising among other great religions, and against our pathological panic for converts.[12] There is a contradiction somewhere: the Church is for all men yet we are to respect other faiths — an open-ended spearhead? The solution to this dilemma is a revived interpretation of the Remnant wherein, whatever the theories, the active working Church, the existential Church, is a vicarious minority. Not indeed an exclusive sect but a well-defined organism which is the servant of the world: a spearhead with sharp edges.[13] We have noted that the community of faith needs identifying characteristics, common prayer and a trinitarian interpretation of life, or it ceases to be a true community, and its spiritual power ceases to be of vicarious significance. The old parish Remnant may be dead or dying, but it must be redesigned and replaced by some other form: the house-church, cell, group or commune. Perhaps such dedicated Christian communities might be called the emerging Remnant; open-ended, ongoing, yet complete and clearly defined. Perhaps we should settle for a spearhead with not blurred but slightly ragged edges, even with serrated edges — no mean weapon!

The new map is now complete. Throughout the *Principles of*

11. *Principles of Christian Theology*, p. 365.
12. *Principles of Christian Theology*, pp. 134–58, 391–5.
13. *See* my *Pastoral Theology: A Reorientation*, pp. 18–25.

Christian Theology Dr. Macquarrie wisely refrained from drawing it: fools rush in . . .

> I have faith in Triune Being.
>
> I risk existence to primordial Being, who through expressive Being lets-be all beings, which through unitive Being, participate in the manifest Being.
>
> I commit myself to expressive Being, who was conceived by unitive Being and born of the Virgin Mary: Jesus Christ, Lord and Word, God and man, Being in being; who suffered under Pontius Pilate, was crucified, dead, buried, He embraced non-being and defeated annihilation. After three days He rose from the dead, and recapitulating all being within himself, reconciling fallen beings with Being, he ascended into Triune Being. Providence and grace, judgment and reconciliation continue.
>
> I place my existence within the community of faith, my friends in Christ, and therefore within the Holy Universal Church, and I hope in faith and love for redemptive consummation. all beings glorified in Being.

Fools rush in . . . Yes it sounds very curious, some donnish joke when the college port has been passed round once too often.

But . . . two vital little points, two important reminders: This is not meant to be a fashionable modern *replacement* of the old creed, but a key, an enlightenment, the necessary spotlight with which to read the old map when you are lost in the dark. Consider both creeds together, and there *may* be some cross-fertilisation.

And, or then, the proof of a map is in its *use*. Is it the old map, or the new map, or both together, that best speeds us on our journey?

What do I do next?

PART THREE

What do I do next?

TEN

What do I do next?

FROM MY premise — I live in this world and I believe in the creed — certain spiritual needs have arisen together with some firm hints as to how they may be met. In other words the two parts of the premise tend to say the same things in different ways, experience endorses credal facts, and our new-map language mediates between them.

My experience tells me that I am at loggerheads with myself and with the environment and that a new harmony is to be sought; the creed says I am a sinner in need of redemption: the new map speaks of alienation, lostness, and reconciliation.

My experience of practical situations is always three-fold; the extended creed says I am made in the image of God who is Trinity: the new map speaks of Triune Being letting-me-be. Situations frequently involve decision in which I experience three factors; the extraneous intangible, the moral reason or conscience, and a deep, supra-rational intuition: the new creed points to providence, sacrifice and discernment of spirits.

I cannot exist alone, life consists of giving and getting from others; old and new creed speak of the Holy Catholic Church and of being-with-others in an on-going incarnation.

Everything speaks of God in whom I put my faith; of Holy Being to whom everything must be risked. And the one absolutely certain thing, certain to both reason and intuition, is that God comes before me; Being before beings. Yet sometimes I sense God, Being is disclosed, but always and obviously on his initiative. The creed says that the Father created me, the Son redeemed me (has? will? might?), and there is a Holy Ghost who is and does various things — Lord of life, giver of life, inspirer of the prophets. All this I firmly believe to be true but it is doubly discursive: it presents me with several isolated facts to think about one by one, and it suggests a God who does various things to me on a series of isolated occasions.

This is now translated as Being lets-be, which brings home in a flash that I have a relation with God which must be continuous, active and unbreakable. This relation is prayer: prayer is relation. Prayer is not something I do, occasionally or without ceasing, but something that is; a relation not to be performed or entered into but to be accepted, recognised, responded to, and above all enjoyed. God acts, God speaks, God lets-be: what do I do next? Can our speculations so far be reduced to some sort of creative order?

As a useful starting point let us re-examine the old order, and see how it meets and falls short of my discovered spiritual needs. This classic scheme of things, the Church's Rule, or *regula*, was tabulated in *Christian Proficiency* thus:[1]

	A	B	C
I.	OFFICE		
II.	EUCHARIST		
III.	PRIVATE PRAYER:	1. Mental Prayer	
		2. Colloquy:	(a) Petition
			(b) Self-examination and Confession
			(c) Intercession
			(d) Thanksgiving— (Almsgiving)
			(e) Adoration
		3. Recollection — (fasting)	

At the risk of some repetition let us recall the similarities and differences between this scheme and that new approach to which our studies point. At the centre of both is the doctrine of the Trinity; both meet all the needs now arising out of experience, but

1. pp. 17–24.

in varying emphases and degrees, so both are adequate and legitimate: the old maps remain *true*, they become unsatisfactory
when related to contemporary cultures. The differences between
old and new is that in three aspects they move in opposite directions. The old *regula* is not tri-theistic but it notoriously courts this
error, and it certainly begins with three Persons, hoping to conclude with unity of substance. The new scheme begins and ends
with Triune Being seen as a unity, even if it has sometimes to
analyse God into three modes or activities, as for example in the
quest for trinitarian choice or decision.

The old *regula* begins in the sanctuary and hopes to move out
into everyday life as habitual recollection; the new starts with
existence — I live in this world — and concentrates life experience
into the eucharistic act.

The old *regula* begins with community and moves out to serve
and nurture individuality; the new begins with I and me and
moves into the fuller existence in community. We may now look in
more detail at the traditional scheme, retaining its strong points
where possible, and attempting to improve upon its weaknesses.

We began with the disclosure of Being in the beings. This experience, however momentary, gave rise to a sense of harmony or
integration which was three-fold: within the self, with creation
and with Being. The creed, -ontology, interpreted this as the activity of God who is Triune Being; in older language it was prevenient grace which hinted at the overcoming of alienation or
lostness, or the disintegration caused by frailty and sin. This contemplative harmony with the beings and with Being is life in
grace, authentic existence, and however difficult to achieve and
maintain it is our ideal. Such experience of grace, or of judgment,
demands a response, an attempt to co-operate with Unitive Being
in his work of striving to restore and maintain in unity all the
beings and existents with Being himself. In old devotional language
we are to seek docility to the Holy Ghost, which is at
bottom — never mind all the degrees and ramifications — contemplative prayer. How are we to go about it?

The old *regula* offers little help so here is an initial lack which
we must try to supply later. Nevertheless the few hints contained in it are of some importance. Its end-product — habitual

recollection — is our starting point, for it means a general continuous relation with God; a commitment, a deep and genuine
awareness of the divine presence which is not necessarily conscious
or articulate. This also comes under the wide heading of contemplation if only because it is certainly not meditative, vocal or discursive. It is the product of which the *regula* is the process, and it is
the unification of a trinitarian system which begins with a strong
stress on the three persons. It is also the end-product of the old
statue polishing process. In the face of tradition, the conception of
Triune Being presents such an anti-discursive simplification, especially when it is seen to manifest itself in letting-be the beings,
that we are tempted to ask whether the venerable process of *regula*
is not somewhat long drawn out. To repeat an analogy I have
used in another context, are we not cutting the lawn with nail-
scissors? There is no doubt that it does the job but is there a less
laborious way?

The *regula* includes self-examination and confession. This also
has the effect of restoring harmony within the self and with Being,
which is again a contemplative process. Starting from existence,
self-examination — or if you like fact-facing humility — springs
spontaneously from the sense of alienation, lostness, or disharmony; in fact from the lack of the sense of Being's disclosure.
The need for forgiveness, for the restoration of unity with Being,
thus springs out of experience and must certainly retain its place in
any new scheme we may propose.

Then comes the need to concentrate existential life into act. The
eucharist does precisely this for it is the focus of harmony between
the beings (bread and wine), existents (the community of faith),
and Being. The eucharist is trinitarian in emphasis — ideally —
since it is offered to the Father, through the Son, in the unity of
the Spirit: it is balanced. It further contains a penitential element,
confession and absolution, which has important implications for
contemplation.

In spite of this ideal trinitarian balance, however, the eucharist
can easily become Christocentric in the narrower and erroneous
sense: the casual observer is likely to gain the impression that the
Christian God is not the Holy Trinity but Christ. So tradition
wisely extends the emphases by introducing the divine office of

transcendental stress and personal devotion centred on the immanent Spirit. But whatever the pastoral wisdom behind this scheme
it leads straight back into the discursive, rather than the contemplative, Trinity. However we hedge the old pattern around
with theological provisos, it cannot avoid a stronger emphasis on
three persons than on one God. On the other hand our new interpretation of experience makes it contemplative not discursive;
to see a tree is to unite with a being let-be by Being rather than to
see a creature made by the Father, redeemed by the Son, and
somehow indwelled by the Spirit. The need to which our argument is moving is for a single, all embracing concentrate of trinitarian experience — which is obviously the eucharist — rather
than for three separable acts, however inter-related they may
be.

As an expression of trinitarian theology, Saturday evensong,
followed by the Sunday eucharist, followed by personal prayer on
Monday, does not make very good sense. Ascetical emphasis on
Father, Son and Holy Ghost, spread over three days is not very
good theology, and it is only by a series of mental and emotional
gymnastics that it stops short of error. Mattins, Holy Communion
and private devotion, following on in rapid succession, is a better
arrangement since the trinitarian emphases tend to flow into one
another and fuse. But this is still not ideal: it is too complex, too
pietistic, and, contrary to tradition, it more or less excludes the
laity if only in terms of time.

What we are pointing to — a single eucharistic concentrate of
trinitarian life — is precisely what is happening in current liturgical development, whether or not these spiritual-theological
factors are clearly understood or considered. For eucharistic experiment invariably begins with a kind of prologue office, or ante-
ante communion, consisting of hymns and canticles of
praise — Gloria, psalmody, and so on — as well as laudatory lections from the Old Testament. Modern liturgies are less regimented and embrace more personal and subjective elements than
of old; the central altar, Westward position and variable inter-
cessions stress this approach. Not only is the eucharist becoming a
true concentrate of trinitarian life, but it is also becoming a concentrate of the old *regula*. And if the eucharist is approached by

way of a sinking into Triune Being, retaining the dominical and personal undertones of the symbols "Father" and "Son", things are further simplified. The achievement of such integrated worship will depend upon the development of a contemplative, trinitarian outlook on life in general. It will begin with the cherry tree and Henry's cup of cold water, it will embrace decision and choice at the disclosure of Being in the beings, it will be the focus and consummation of life. And it will be as near to the trinitarian ideal of worship as human frailty permits.

Parallel with this liturgical reform is a tedious and long drawn out movement towards the revision and simplification of the divine office, of which the idea of a eucharistic prologue of corporate praise is a disjointed part. There would seem to be every theological justification for saying, with the utmost simplicity, that these were one and the same thing: that the eucharistic prologue of praise *is* the daily office. Tradition and theology agree that the corporate praise of the divine transcendence constitutes the essential purpose of the office; this is here fulfilled within the eucharist, and therefore within the Trinity.

The pastoral implications are equally important. In, and since, *Christian Proficiency*, I have firmly upheld the Anglican insistence that the divine office — "daily throughout the year" — is no clerical preserve but the prayer of the Church, and therefore of all the faithful. But I must reluctantly admit that so long as this remains a complex structure, involving several books, Calendars and Lectionaries, the bulk of the faithful are unlikely to use it. The eucharistic prologue-office, consisting of the Lord's Prayer, collect and canticle of praise, is the office at its efficient theological minimum, and were it boldly authorised I have no doubt that the faithful would gladly embrace it: it would become the corporate concentrate of the disclosure of transcendent Being, as well as a tangible bond of unity among all Christians.[2]

It has always been a firm principle of traditional spirituality that personal devotion is uniquely personal, since no two people are alike. There have, indeed, been periods and schools of thought wherein disciplined regimentation, clear-cut method and tech-

2. *See* pp. 112f. above.

nique, have been thrust upon a docile laity, to the detriment of prophecy and freedom of spirit. But even if such an approach has agreed with some cultural patterns, it has generally been subjected to criticism and distrust. The corporate-individual balance is always difficult to maintain, and it is clear that the contemporary emphasis is upon the personal and existential. The ordinary divisions of private prayer, therefore, as tabulated in column C of the *regula*, may be seen as foci of experience and left alone. To what extent individual persons require such to be ordered into rules and timetables can be left to their own judgment.

There remains mental prayer, which has played an enormous part in past tradition, and which now looks like taking a poor second place to contemplative forms. It is worth recalling why this transformation of values has taken place. Firstly because substantive doctrinal statements are discursive and analytic; existential-ontological statements are synthetic and contemplative. The trinity of Father, Son and Holy Ghost, demands to be considered, thought about, analysed. Triune Being demands to be looked at, absorbed, grasped, sunk into.

The second reason for this transference of values is yet to be considered: it is because in tradition contemplation has been treated in a narrow and "advanced" way, which leaves only mental prayer available to the less gifted, "ordinary" Christian. Soon we hope to show that there is such a thing as "ordinary" contemplative prayer.

Meditation, however, is not entirely eliminated, for central to my experienced needs is the ability to choose, and my decisions, advancing or diminishing existence, are to be made with reference to the activity of Triune Being. Central to this is the mind and ethic of Christ as revealed in sacred scripture, and yet the Bible is by no means confined to this. The Old Testament in particular has a good deal to teach about both the providential action of God in history and about discernment through prophetic wisdom. We have spoken of the personal and contemporary "Exodus", and of the prophetic inspiration which arises not infrequently in the wilderness of silence.

In tradition, moreover, meditation is almost as ambiguous as contemplation, for it can mean anything from some tight method,

minutely detailed and regulated, to reading the Bible. Louis
Bouyer widens the traditional *Lectio Divina* into many different
approaches, from this laborious exercise concerning a single text to
reading through a whole book at an arm-chair sitting.[3] We are
almost returning to Caroline England when this freedom worked
miracles and inclined towards the latter method. *Christian
Proficiency* inclined towards the former method, and all we need
insist upon in a new scheme of prayer is absolute freedom from all
method. If we are to achieve a growing insight into the mind of
Christ, as central to Triune activity, the Bible must be part of life;
to be read thoroughly on occasion and picked up casually on
others. Decision-making will interact with it, and although temperament will dictate Bible reading schedules, or their absence,
meditation need form no part of a rigid framework, neither does
the daily office require scriptural lections.

Starting from our premise — I live in this world and I believe in
the creed — the old Benedictine-Anglican *regula* is still valid. In
spite of under and over emphases it provides for the fullness of
Christian living, and its rejection, or revision, or substitution by
some other scheme, is necessitated not only by theology but by
culture. It breaks down under the pressures of modern life and it is
unattractive to the contemporary mind. Its still considerable advantage is that any committed Christian, professor or schoolgirl,
bishop or banker, can fully embrace it at once, without fuss, preparation or too much theology. To embrace it perfectly is a life's
work, to embrace it proficiently is open to all, and progress is
assured.

Its disadvantages are discursiveness, complexity, and to the
modern temperament, artificiality. A further difficulty is that it is
rigidly tied in with the liturgical calendar, which, despite its
obvious usefulness, is again discursive rather than contemplative.
Since we live in time some temporal framework to prayer is required, but if Saturday evensong, Sunday communion and private prayer on Monday is unsatisfactory then so also are the long
drawn out stresses of the liturgical year. To celebrate the Incarnation on Christmas Day, the Atonement on Good Friday, the
Ascension six weeks later, the feast of the Holy Ghost on Whit-

3. *Introduction to Spirituality* (Darton, 1964), pp. 45–55.

sunday and that of the Trinity the week after: all this hardly helps towards an integrated, contemplative view of total life in Triune Being. The alternation of fast and festival can constitute a healthy discipline and a liberation from the slavery to feeling, but it can also appear to be absurdly artificial. In life penitence alternates with praise as Being is disclosed in judgment and grace, and providential activity is totally heedless of the ecclesiastical calendar. If providence, the activity of primordial Being, manifests enormous benevolence on Ash Wednesday, there is nothing very devout in being gloomy about it.

This follows current trends, for the calendar is being revised and simplified; the emphases on Lent and Advent are shortened and diminished, and the conservative is invited to look at the theological and cultural factors behind this revision before he puts it all down to slackness and decadence.

A final criticism of the traditional *regula* combines a strength with a weakness. It can be immediately embraced by anyone, and growth in spirit is interpreted as a gradual tending towards habitual recollection, with its necessary concomitant of moral improvement. Progress means to pray and live better, and this is a healthy reaction against the heirarchical ladders, scales and categories so beloved of the medieval writers. Personal prayer patterns may indeed change in type as well as in degree; meditation may give way to contemplation, discursive colloquy to silent adoration. But such developments are left to God's leading and are not to be striven for: to pray better may or may not imply to pray differently. So far so good, but this approach, healthy in itself, omits the equally traditional principle of periodicy; that life in general and spiritual life in particular moves in fairly well defined phases. Strongly resisting any sort of monastic professionalism, any modern approach to prayer must nevertheless take some note of this principle. Our new system will take on the character of a phased structure, beginning with a serious catechumenate — which is a venerable tradition indeed — and possibly following with something like the old *regula* as foundation for the main business of life in Triune Being. If this looks like complicating, rather than simplifying things, it is only because it is true to life for human existence is never easily tabulated: this

I

indeed is the charge of artificiality against the old *regula*.

The new approach to which we are leading is indeed a simplification in both common and technical senses. It is simpler in so far as there are far fewer acts, duties, heading, sub-headings, schedules and so on. It is also more technically simple in that it is less discursive, and there are obvious, rather than theologically calculable, inter-relations between its parts. Because of this inherent simplicity it is more difficult to reduce to plan, we are no longer concerned with a rule of life based on God the Holy Trinity, but with trinitarian life in its fullness and depth. It is more readily described than tabulated, but the time has come for us to attempt both.

ELEVEN

The New Map as Prayer

THE SPIRITUALITY to which our speculations are pointing is more of a life than a rule, more of a journey than a map, or more precisely, a journey in which the map, though useful, remains in the background. The credal map cannot be discarded but the new map invites adventurous risk amongst the by-ways rather than a laborious trudge along the main road. Its simplest counterpart to the old *regula* is depicted thus:

Habitual

    Recollection — *focused* in Acts:

        (i)   Colloquy

       (ii)   Bible Reading   *focused* in:

      (iii)   Eucharistic —
              prologue — office

                           office —
                         EUCHARIST

That is the old *regula*, with nothing omitted but much simplified, and with the order reversed. To make descriptive sense of it, however, this map needs to be re-drawn on a larger scale:

Existence in
Awareness of
Being——disclosed as: ————————*focused in Acts* — *FOCUS*

```
T
          Grace (contemplative   —   Adoration    —      E
R              harmony)          —   Thanksgiving —
                                                  — p    U
I         Judgment (alienation:  —   Penitence    — r
               lostness)         —   Confession   — o    C
N                                                 — l
          Situations (choice)    —   Petition     — o    H
I                                —   Intercession — g
                                                  — u    A
T                                                 — e
                                                  — ..   R
Y——————————— by:  Providence      —   T           — o
                                  —   R           — f    I
                 Moral doctrine — —   I           — f
                 (Bible reading)  —   N           — i    S
                                  —   I           — c
                 Discernment      —   T           — e    T
                 (Silence)        —   Y
```

That looks pretty terrifying, but it expresses a simplification. It is a fairly large scale map to aid in the description of what Christian life is. It is not a list of duties to be undertaken but a plan to indicate how Holy Being discloses himself and it offers some direction to our response. Contrary to the old *regula*, we have here not a series of columns which might be made to interact but a process of concentration; all the lists and columns deal with precisely the same thing — life in Triune Being, but in varying degrees of experience and concentration. The eucharist is not something that enters into that life, or which forms a part of it; it is the final focus of the life itself, it is all the rest in concentrate and consummation. Our fundamental purpose and method, however, is description[1] and our attempt to tabulate the new approach to prayer, to redraw the new spiritual-theological map, is for this purpose only.

1. *Principles of Christian Theology*, pp. 30–32.

The starting point, existence in awareness of Being, is our initial premise, I live in this world and I believe in the creed, and both parts of this statement are trinitarian. Whether interpreted in terms of religion, anthropology, psychology, sociology, or anything else, human life is triune, for it comprises the impingement of transcendent powers, immanent inspiration or discernment, and the mediation of sensory things. The examples given in previous chapters may be illuminated by looking at any serious novel, or any historical sequence of events. The hero of the detective story looks for clues, which mediate discernment, creating a pattern of prophetic thought, and then something happens, something extraneous, an impingement from outside, disturbing the logical sequence of things. More sophisticated stories deal with psychological relationships, giving rise to feelings, emotions, awe, wonder, anxiety, tragedy. Discernment, decision, choice is mediated through people, and then again something extraneous happens, something beyond the control of the characters, suddenly transcendent.

It follows that Being is also to be conceived as triune, and the creed explains the Christian interpretation of this revealed truth. But in order to make this supreme revelation of God one's own, to assimilate or, as Macquarrie says, "appropriate" it,[2] it must impinge on existence as a contemplative, instead of, or at least as well as, a discursive fact. It must be grasped as well as understood. The way towards such contemplative recollection is still our great task, and the most serious omission from the old scheme: it must still be left until later. Nevertheless, the reinterpretation of God the Holy Trinity in the language of Being itself offers considerable assistance, and this is underlined by the very experience of Being's self-disclosure and manifestation.

Although an over simplification, the second column explains that this disclosure of the presence of Being is itself three-fold. It is manifested as grace, and as benevolent providence, which is to some extent experienced as contemplative harmony within the self, with beings and existents, and with Being itself. The old language of devotion describes such experience as of peace, or

2. *Principles of Christian Theology*, p. 31.

simplicity, or loving regard, or affectiveness, and its natural concentrate is focused on adoration and thanksgiving. Such acts of prayer can be private and personal, but they can also be concentrated into the divine office, here rightly shared with the community of faith. On the new map this is the eucharistic prologue reduced to the Lord's Prayer, possibly a collect, and canticles and psalms of praise. Against weighty tradition it follows that the moment of the disclosure of Being as grace is the supreme occasion for offering the divine office, for now *Te Deum* and *Benedicite*, *Jubilate Deo* and *Gloria in Excelsis*, burst forth spontaneously. This is the revealed moment, the *kairos* of praise, not six-thirty a.m. and six-thirty p.m. precisely. It must also follow that "private" recitation of the office (which in no real way detracts from its corporate significance[3]) has considerable advantage over the office "in choir". Since the office will also be included, as prologue, in the eucharist, it is no longer valid to regard private recitation at the revealed time as a poor second-best.

There is still much to be said for order and discipline, the known disclosure of Being may be rare, yet he must be praised in act. Let us suggest that for proficient and commited Christians, the eucharist-prologue-office should be offered daily, more than once if need be, and leave it at that. It will concentrate and recall the gracious disclosure of Being, whenever that last occurred, but there is no particular point in the old devotional idea of an early morning office. This discipline claims to put God first, which sounds devout enough; in practice it is also a dutiful way of getting prayer over and done with so that we can get on with other things!

Being is also disclosed as judgment, qualified by the sense of alienation, lostness, disharmony within selfhood, society and environment, and this experience is concentrated into acts of penitence, self-examination and confession. We have agreed to ride loosely upon the ways and methods of these concentrated acts, maintaining my point in *Christian Proficiency* that private and sacramental confession are correlates not alternatives.[4] But the disclosure of Being as judgment, the seemingly malevolent action

3. *See* my *The Rock and the River* (Hodder, 1965), pp. 105–11.
4. pp. 110–15.

of providence — God's transcendent awkwardness — may still be a *kairos* of praise to mature and stable Christians. We have spoken of the judgmental disclosure of Being as the experience of being overjoyed with disappointment; of a subtle discernment of possibilities in a providential situation which are not immediately apparent.[5] This is a true act of faith and could give rise to a spontaneous desire to praise; the eucharistic-prologue-office would again be appropriate.

Whether by grace or judgment, Being is disclosed in the situation, in the providential pattern of events. And the mediation of this disclosure is by a complex of beings and existents, things and people, or environment and society. Concentrated into acts of prayer, this experience leads into petition and intercession, which is the first step to decision, for Being disclosed through situations invariably implies choice. Intercession and petition may be important factors in reaching the situational decision, but they are not enough; reference has to be made to the trinitarian pattern of the divine activity in life. To put it another way, petition and intercession must themselves be trinitarian. This has been discussed as a complex of the infinite possibilities of transcendent providence, of the mind of Christ expressed in moral doctrine, and of the discernment associated with a docility to the indwelling Spirit. Proficiency in trinitarian choice demands, therefore, a familiarity with the biblical revelation and some exercise in discerning the leading of the Spirit. On our new spiritual-theological map these accomplishments are attained by Bible reading and by a creative use of silence. Details may still be left to the various needs of individuals, but Bible reading and the experimental use of silence need to enter into life in fairly large doses, at least in the initial stages. Existential principles, but no methods are involved, and we may speak of Bible reading, Bible study, meditation, mental prayer, silence, waiting on God, listening to the Spirit, or the prayer of simplicity, without it making very much difference. For the tidy minded, two hours' weekly attention to the Bible, which lies around the house for the rest of the time, and the same sort of period devoted to silence, might be a reasonable suggestion. How, when and where are matters of no importance.

5. *See* p. 86 above.

The whole is finally concentrated in the focus of the eucharist, which includes its prologue-office, for the eucharist is the creed in dramatic action, the Christian life of trinitarian faith in microcosm. That is said often enough but, after the old order, more as a remote ideal than as an attainable fact. Once we begin from an existential-ontological standpoint the ideal comes within reach, for all acts of prayer are concentrates of life. It is also frequently stated that the eucharist has a double, two-way, action, in which God not only enters our world and life but also lifts them into himself. The eucharist is not only a channel of grace, of power and strength for the future, but a consummation of the past. This fits exactly with Macquarrie's new map theology, for the eucharist is the existential moment, the focus of temporality which constitutes existence; the bringing into unity of the dimensions of past, present and future. "Acceptance of the remembered past, commitment to an overarching possibility of the future, and openness in the present to both of these."[6] This is the eucharistic attitude of tradition, and it underlines the importance of seeing that creation, reconciliation and consummation, are to be understood, not as successive activities but as distinguishable aspects of God's great unitary action.[7]

Pastoral and devotional tradition, however, have become heavily weighted on the preparatory-future aspects of eucharistic worship; it is a channel of grace which equips the communicant with strength to face the future. This is a legitimate aspect, but only one, and it has taken hold through the long tradition of celebrating the eucharist early in the morning. The natural thing to do in the morning is to prepare for the coming day, but with the present popularity of evening celebrations the devotional emphasis is likely to be reversed; the eucharist becomes a consummation of what has gone before, a thanksgiving for past blessings. But the ideal is not so much consummation as concentration, focus, or the eucharistic achievement of the existential moment. Perhaps the city guild-churches, with their celebrations at mid-day, have stumbled upon a lost principle of pastoral-theology. Our new interpretation not only fits well with the best

6. *Principles of Christian Theology*, p. 320.
7. *Principles of Christian Theology*, pp. 246-8.

traditions of eucharistic worship but offers practical help in its attainment. This is especially so when the essential trinitarianism of the eucharist is supported, and rendered contemplative, by reference to Triune Being. With this approach the arguments about time, morning, evening or mid-day become irrelevant: it is focus or concentrate of total existence.

Again for the tidy minded, or perhaps for the old-fashioned, we are now in a position to list the acts, or duties, of committed Christian life. To adopt the traditional order, there is the eucharist which includes the divine office by way of prologue. Let us assist at this central, corporate and focal art of worship say once or twice a week, but frequency must vary with circumstances and personal choice. The office will be said, by rule and duty, say once to three times daily, and this will be from memory without books, lectionaries, or other impedimenta. But the office might be much more frequent as Holy Being is disclosed in grace and judgment. Acts of personal prayer will arise out of experience, and must also be variable by circumstance: those who like rules may make them, and it would be wise. There must be a significant period of silence, and another with the Bible, each week. This is no hollow duty but the necessary preparation for choice which makes the integrated self. It does not matter when any of these acts take place, but while we are being nice and old-fashioned perhaps Sunday afternoon would be appropriate.

Prayer is relationship in life, so the development of contemplative awareness, harmony, a sinking into Being, remains the crux of the matter, and this leads us to the two admitted difficulties of the new map scheme. The next chapters will look seriously at contemplation; the present one must conclude with the complication we have called the phased structure of Christian life. The great advantage of the old *regula* is that anyone can embrace it at once. A certain amount of guidance is sensible, and possibly necessary, but there is no need for any arduous preparation. Anyone can do it badly, and gradually improve. The new-map spirituality, on the other hand, demands an initial period of preparation, a catechumenate, which pays heed to the classic principle of periodicy. This means something like a three-phased structure from Christian initiation to proficiency. It may be tabulated thus:

but with the usual proviso that all such schemes look, and are, tidier than life.

A. *CATECHUMENATE:*
> Personal Guidance:
>> The Creed in old and new maps
>> Biblical Introduction
>
>> Mental Prayer
>> Eucharistic — prologue — office
>> EUCHARISTIC WORSHIP
>> Exercises in Contemplation

B. *BEGINNERS:*
> as A., reduced and concentrated
> (daily lections)
> Guidance within the Community of Faith
> Exercises and experiments in Contemplation
> and Silence
> Experiments in choice

C. *PROFICIENCY:*
> (as previously described)

That also looks frightening, but having admitted a complication as compared with the immediate embrace of the old *regula* certain palliatives might fairly be considered. I have tried to explain the genius of the old scheme in a way that is frequently applied to the eucharist; that it can serve, sanctify, and be immediately embraced by all of faith and goodwill; that it proves satisfactory and creative to professor and peasant, saint and schoolgirl. Nevertheless both history and pastoral-theology point to the latter groups as those to which it is mainly directed. The Rule of St. Benedict itself was "a little rule for beginners", the Book of Common Prayer is pastorally directed to a newly emancipated yet largely illiterate laity.

I have also insisted that — thank God — theology is not necessary for sanctification, and let us hope and pray for a continuing stream of "unlettered" saints. But if sanctity flows out from the *regula* without articulate theology, peasants, schoolgirls and the unlettered will need guidance which must take on a certain authoritarian flavour.

In spite of its essential virtue, therefore, the *regula* conflicts with the contemporary outlook at three cultural points. Although technically simple it is rigidly plodding, its results are slow to appear and it implies an unpopular regimentation. Secondly, although academic learning can be both sterile and exaggerated, and although modern people can get bored and frustrated by it, we live in an intensely theological age. Theology is popular, and insistence upon its unimportance may no longer be the most charitable approach to the modern convert. Thirdly, although sane guidance is always acceptable anything remotely like clerical authoritarianism must now be rejected. The *regula* implies such an approach, however alleviated by the sanity of the English pastoral tradition. Moreover, we have found serious conflicts between the old "virtue" of obedience and the new spiritual and trinitarian virtue of choice and risk. Guidance remains, but transformed in a way which renders the *regula* more difficult to apply.

The catechumenate, therefore, although a little forbidding at first sight, may prove to be the kind of thing that modern converts desire. It is also the type of thing they partially get, in confirmation preparation, group discussions and so on, but I am suggesting a return to the catechetical instructions of tradition; more real, meaningful and thorough, and firmly based both on modern theologies of Being and involving the prayer and life-pattern which flows therefrom.

The schedule for the catechumenate, as tabulated, is obviously variable and experimental, but I think it contains the elements necessary to proficiency: it might be worth some further description. By the old pattern, one embraced the *regula* because of the dictates of the Church; theological backing and interpretation were forthcoming if they were requested, but this was not necessary. Once the *regula* was embraced, guidance helped towards the correct ascetical emphases proper to each part, and this ultimately led into a trinitarian interpretation of God as he was experienced and served. The shortcomings of this scheme have already been pointed out: in spite of a general trinitarian balance in life and prayer, tri-theistic tendencies were never wholly eliminated.[8] The new premise — I live in this world and I believe in the creed — implies that I have some general understanding of what the creed means, and although greater depths of meaning will be revealed throughout life, a clear comprehension is initially necessary. Any understanding of the creed by contemporary people will necessitate interpretation in modern idiom. This will probably employ existential categories in some form, and I choose John Macquarrie: there are others. This seemingly intellectual process — translating substance language into terms of existence and Being — has a profound, and almost immediate effect on transforming discursive meditation into contemplative prayer.

Nevertheless mental prayer retains its place at this stage, since it is necessary to plumb the biblical depths, and it remains a factor in the process of entering into the mind of Christ. Under the old, non-theological scheme, this could be supported by some introduction to biblical theology, and an acquaintance with the principles of Christian ethics, but these were optional extras; direction and confession could replace them. Under the new scheme biblical and moral theology will have their place in some part, the contemporary outlook will demand them, and they have a necessary place in the crux of Christian living: trinitarian choice.

The eucharistic-prologue-office has its place in the catechumenate, as of course does eucharistic worship, but these are much reduced. In fact a problem could arise at the catechumenate stage because formal acts of prayer are reduced too much This is why I have suggested that the *regula*, or a sensible modification of it, might still form a valuable foundation at this stage. A slightly longer office, with biblical lections, and fairly regular periods of colloquy — seen as concentrates of life — could form an efficient framework which could be dispensed with later.

The attainment of a contemplative harmony, three-fold and triune, forms the crux and focus of the whole thing. And I hope it will prove an exciting experiment: the acquisition of a contemplative outlook in triune Being is a spiritual adventure, not a

8. *See* my *Pastoral Theology: a Reorientation*, pp. 192–204.

burdensome duty, a life to be lived abundantly, not a problem to be solved.

Little need be said about phase B, since it is largely a concentrate of phase A, and the two will overlap and fuse. Phase C is the proficient result of everything this book has attempted to explain, suggest, and describe. The important principle underlying the phased scheme is that of periodicy; Christian life changes in type as well as degree, our new maps not only lead us steadily along a straight and narrow road but may also force us to change direction. This is within the classic tradition, but it is accentuated by the centrality of choice which involves risk. Everything that has flowed from our approach implies bold spiritual adventure, great leaps of faith, interspersed throughout the dutiful trudge.

Finally, if this phased structure of Christian life appears as a burdensome complication, further palliatives now present themselves. In dealing with the initial phases I have considered the needs of new converts. So all I have really suggested is an up-dated preparation for confirmation, and up-dated in two ways. First, in so far as things are put into contemporary terms and idiom; secondly, in that we are treating Christian initiation with the seriousness that the post-Christendom Church requires. The old six-week crash-course of confirmation classes, mainly aimed at children in their early 'teens is plainly a thing of the past. If, on the other hand, we are dealing with committed Christians who are searching for a more meaningful and contemporary interpretation of life and prayer, then they are obviously through phase A, and probably B, already. They will have a thorough understanding of the old creed, a familiarity with the Bible, and with the usual acts of prayer culminating in the eucharist. If they are in the habit of using the divine office, even in some modified form, then this is only what we have suggested as the heart of phase B. The great difference between 1959 and today (possibly with *Honest to God* in 1963 as a watershed) is the revived interest in, and demand for, theology. *Christian Proficiency* was written under the assumption that serious Christians wanted to enrich their experience of God through prayer, but with a minimum of theology. They wanted to be guided and coached in what to do and how to do it; they did

not want to theorise about it. I do not think that this applies any
longer.

There are differences in make-up and temperament, however,
and this poses a dilemma. The theologically interested, the intellectual if you like, will be excited by Macquarrie, and the new
insights he gives to the creed. The reinterpretation of a persons-
substance-trinity into Triune Being will immediately suggest a
contemplative rather than a meditative interpretation of religious
experience. On the other hand it is the non-intellectual, the poet
and lover, who is naturally contemplative. The former, by nature,
is discursive, logical and analytic; the latter is not interested in
such processes, but he is potentially contemplative. Here is the
modern difficulty with the faithful unlettered, and at long last the
time has come to try to resolve the problem in terms of both
experience and theology. It will remain, in practice, a question of
pastoral guidance of individuals: the pastor at least still needs
theology. Perhaps the crux, which is itself part of existential culture, is that the modern scientific-intellectual, especially in theology, is so frequently a poet-lover as well.

TWELVE

The Meaning of Contemplation

THROUGHOUT this study the word *contemplation* has been used in an unusual and ambiguous way. This is inevitable because it is an unusually ambiguous word, and even at the risk of a certain pedantry its various shades of meaning must be unravelled in order that we may get down to the practical business of contemplative prayer. The meaning of the word may be examined under four headings, clearly distinguishable yet inter-related in varying degrees, and these we shall call the *psychological*, the *religious*, the *Christian-trinitarian*, and the *mystical*.

Under the first heading, the *psychological*, contemplative experience is associated with ideas like personal integration; harmony in life, environment and relationships; mental health and emotional balance; wholeness, completeness, stability and maturity. The psychological opposite of contemplation is a disordered, alienated self, a sense of lostness in the universe, and finally I suppose, schizophrenia.

These words and phrases take us straight back to Macquarrie's interpretation of existence and selfhood. Human existence implies a tension between various polarities and this gives rise to a fundamental disorder, which is described by the words just used: imbalance, alienation, lostness. This condition may be redressed by decisions which seek to harmonise the polarities of existence. "Authentic selfhood implies the attainment of a unified existence, in which potentialities are actualised in an orderly manner and there are no loose ends or alienated areas."[1] That is a fair description of the initial contemplative state, and it ties in with the more general existential insistence on the unity of being; authentic

---

1. *Principles of Christian Theology*, p. 67.

existence means commitment of one's whole self, integrated and unified. It is things like commitment, purpose, love and choice which produce the contemplative state on a human, psychological plane.

This psychological experience becomes *religious* as soon as the fundamental disorder within the self, in relation to the created environment, and in society, is seen to flow from a more radical alienation from God. Disorder, imbalance, alienation, lostness, now become sin, and this is almost exactly what St. Augustine means by concupiscence. Its opposite is contemplative integration, which may be called righteousness or holiness, or indeed, wholeness. Now in view of what is soon to follow it is important to notice how this elementary psycho-religious idea of harmony or integration — for we have yet to reach the fullness of Christian-trinitarianism — is taken over by the classical Christian tradition. As against discursive meditation, contemplation in its initial stage is simply an integrated, simple awareness of God. Adolphe Tanquery describes it as "the simplification of our intellectual and affective acts".[2] Bossuet calls it "the prayer of simplicity".[3] To St. Teresa it is "the prayer of recollection . . . it is called recollection because the soul collects together all the faculties and enters within itself to be with God".[4] That is only another way of describing the tensions, imbalances, and polarities of existence being re-collected into an integrated harmony; and that is existential commitment. St. Thomas Aquinas defines contemplation as "a simple intellectual view of the truth, superior to reasoning and accompanied by admiration".[5] But the variation of phrase describing this primary, simple or "acquired" contemplation, is almost infinite: it is the prayer of "simple regard", "loving regard", "simple unity", or just "of simplicity". It all points to much the same thing and ties in with the more popular, dictionary meaning of the word: simply to look, gaze, pay attention to, or concentrate on something, but always "with one's whole being".

2. *The Spiritual Life* (Soc. of St. John Evangelist 1933; Mercier, 1938), p. 605.
3. *See* de Caussade, *On Prayer*, Dialogue VII.
4. *Way of Perfection*, Chapter 28.
5. *Summa*, IIa, IIae, q. 180, a. 1.6.

This psycho-religious experience becomes Christian when the ultimate alienation — sin — is seen to be overcome by Christ's redemption, and when God is understood as the Holy Trinity. But the substantive-person language of the creed detracts from any unified, or contemplative sense of the Trinity. The formula is discursive, theological and intellectual, whatever the affective implications of the words "Father" and "Son". This looks like that unnecessary complication so often associated with the central doctrine of the Christian faith: What is wrong with the second form of contemplation just described? What is wrong with natural harmony associated with God? Why drag in difficult ideas like the Trinity?

First of course, because the revealed God of the Christians is Trinity and nothing less rich will do. Even as we strive after integration and simplicity, the word "God" in itself dwindles away in vagary. More important is that only the doctrine of the Trinity can permit, interpret and make sense of, a genuinely contemplative experience of harmony in and with creation. Only the Trinity of Creator, Redeemer and immanent Spirit, can validate harmony within one's self, with the environment and in society, as genuine *prayer*. It is the interpretation of God as Triune Being which both enriches and integrates this experience.

Let us break off at this point and look at a couple of examples of this progression. Suppose a happily married family man has created a garden around his home; today he has tended it, weeded some flower beds, clipped the hedges and mown the lawn. Pleasantly tired he bathes, dresses in clean clothes, takes a deck-chair and a pint of beer and sits on his newly shaven lawn. He just rests, and one is tempted to introduce the biblical word *anapauo* — I rest, for this is the contemplative consummation of all creative activity. It is the Sabbath rest of God on the seventh day of creation[6] — but we are moving too fast. The man sits and thinks, then just sits, and contemplates: he is at home with himself, with his little bit of creation, in love with his wife and at one with his children. Everything in the garden, is, literally and figuratively, lovely: he does not think, or plan, or worry: he is in a state of

6. Genesis 2, 2, *see* pp. 165–6 below.

K

contemplation, naturally, humanly, psychologically. In spite of the rather pretentious word contemplation, this experience is common enough and comparatively shallow; it is little more than a general peace of mind, perhaps a quiet conscience, a sense of human well-being, a spirit of contentment.

Recalling William Temple we can say that this experience, however ordinary, is religious experience, or prayer, just in so far as its subject is a religious man. When the idea of God is introduced the whole scene takes on a new depth; there is a hint of purpose, final and eternal purpose behind everything, garden, flowers, hedges, wife, children. There is a deep inarticulated thanksgiving, an adoring praise: now we may speak freely and accurately of contemplative prayer. In virtue of human psychological make-up, this experience will probably take on vague trinitarian implications. An idea of creation, and of a transcendent creator will come to mind; so will that of an immanent, life-giving spirit, perhaps some sort of fertility symbol; and the whole environment, the material things of it, will themselves mediate between them. If the man loves a particular tree, if such a tree sums up his experience in focus, becomes a concentrate of it, and he wants to call it a sacred tree then, at this second stage, there is nothing to stop him.

If the man is a Christian he will be appraised of a revealed explanation of all this, he will be able to make sense of it and eventually to harness it with specific acts of prayer, shared with the community of faith. Meanwhile he will be tempted to think, discursively and meditatively, about how the creator is known as heavenly Father, God Almighty. Jesus Christ somehow redeems, beautifies, glorifies this total environment; garden, home, wife, family, giving it all a new unity and a new splendour. And the Holy Ghost indwells it all, Lord and giver of Life, Paraclete, Comforter, Inspirer of prayer and Leader into all truth.

This is a necessary complication and it could be called a retrogression, for we have moved back from a contemplative experience to a discursive soliloquy. We have moved from prayer to theology which is going in the wrong direction. The theology is nevertheless necessary if we are to introduce trinitarian richness without sinking back into deistic gods of thunder and sacred trees. But there is a way over this hurdle. Our contemplative experience can be reinterpreted in terms of Being letting-be the beings; of primordial Being moving out through expressive Being to love and let-be; of unitive Being striving to restore, reconcile, unite, bring into harmony, all the beings with Being. This not only explains and interprets but induces the contemplate state, it deepens and sustains it. The man not only sinks back into his deckchair, he sinks into Being. Being grasps him and lifts him into the Trinity. All the beings point to Being, even his beer, and like coffee and cold water, the taste and smell and feel of beer is part of his contemplative state because it is a participation in the sacred humanity of expressive Being made Man.

One further example, for which let us return to the nuptial analogy of the classical tradition. The man proposes marriage and the lady accepts. Here is a psychological union, a contemplative harmony in which the total being of two existent selves meets at a point. There are no loose ends; intellect, senses, emotions, hopes, fears and ambitions, all fuse into an integrated simplicity, and the whole universe joins in, focused in an embrace. There is no discursive reasoning, neither is interested in the accomplishments, characteristics or qualities of the other. Even at this stage, their love could be described by the definitions of contemplative prayer just mentioned: it is of "simple regard", a "simple unity" of "loving regard", the experience is re-collective in St. Teresa's sense.

Given faith in God, the experience becomes religious. There is a deeper purpose, a deeper meaning, a new depth of awe and wonder, a fearful joy. This is the contemplative *kairos*, the existential moment which is neither past, present nor future but a new synthesis of time which is close to the eternal.

Given Christianity God draws near in trinitarian action. The lovers may think, if they wish, of a heavenly Father watching benignly over them, of the presence of Jesus Christ, risen and glorified, and of the Holy Ghost, brooding over and indwelling them both: but in all probability they will *not* wish to theologise! Even with the most devout and committed Christians, such theologising is unreal. Reinterpreted, Being has let-be, Being is letting-be, God is love. The total situation is gloriously providential, God is at work. And the very embrace of the lovers is a participation in expressive Being incarnate; the embrace itself, like the taste of cold water and coffee is christological, it is religious experience, a participation in the sacred humanity. The contemplative embrace, the existential moment of unity, the *kairos* of harmony, is the work of unitive Being. Being lets-be, and a human, psychological experience enters into the depths of unfathomable joy, of joy transcendent because it indwells, partaking of Christ's reconciliation.

I have offered these examples in order to show that something which can validly be called contemplation arises out of existence itself. At the first stage it is a psychological or natural experience, which nevertheless has some affinity with elementary, or "acquired" contemplation as it is described in the classic text-books. The difference between psychological adjustment and contemplative prayer is infinite, they are two distinct things, yet up to now we have found some kind of continuity. Psychological ideas like alienation, lostness and emotional balance have at least an analogical relation with religious experiences such as penitence, sin and reconciliation.

When we come to the fourth category of contemplation, the *mystical*, we move into a different world altogether. And it is a very frightening one for now any semblance of continuity with ordinary experience falls to pieces. We enter into the modern equivalent of that old bugbear of ascetical theology: the "double standard".[7] But this is no longer a distinction between monk and secular, priest and layman, but between everyday Christianity and the esoteric, professional world of the text-books; ordinary Christians, however committed in faith, say their prayers, assist at the eucharist, and mediate: contemplation is reserved strictly for the specially gifted, the "advanced", the near-sanctified, and it is achieved, or rather given by God, only after a lifetime of terrifying struggle. This is the common use of the word contemplation in traditional spirituality, and it has one characteristic which sets it apart from the other legitimate meanings we have just described.

7. *See* K. E. Kirk, *The Vision of God* (Harper & Row, 1966; Hodder, 1966), Lecture V, ii, Additional Notes, M. N.

In this tradition the object of contemplation is always God, un-mediated by symbols or creatures.

Nevertheless, this tradition, strongly entrenched as it is, is not wholly unopposed from within the Church itself. Hans von Balthasar puts it thus:

A profound cleavage runs through the history of Christian spirituality. On the one hand, we have the protagonists of a platonic kind of contemplation which strives after contact with the "naked" truth, a direct "touching" of the essence of God, albeit in the night of the senses and spirit and in a simple non-conceptual awareness of God's presence; it aims at a corresponding abstraction from the sensible, first from the external senses, then from the imagination, and finally from all finite ideas bound up, as they are, with the world. On the other hand, we have the advocates of a contemplation dependent on the sensible images and concepts of the Gospel and the whole historical course of salvation. St. Bernard and St. Francis, to some extent, and St. Ignatius in particular, were opposed to the dominant traditional conception, and insisted on a concrete type of contemplation using the imagination and, indeed, the five senses. As a general rule, the Platonisers considered this kind of contemplation only useful for beginners, as they did the discursive Ignatian method employing the various faculties of the soul (representation of the object, rational consideration, application of the will and affections). They considered that the methods using sense and reason had to lead up to the "prayer of simplicity" or of "recollection" or of the "heart", in which all that is exterior and manifold in imagery and thinking becomes progressively interiorised to give place to rest in the presence of the object sought, while images and thoughts, if not wholly excluded, are relegated to the background.[8]

A good many more anti-platonic authorities could be cited — Hugh of St. Victor, John Scotus Erigina, Julian of Norwich, St. Thomas Aquinas — and nothing could be more tedious

8. *Prayer* (Chapman, 1963), p. 211.

than yet another academic discussion about contemplation as "in-fused" or "acquired", "immediate" or mediated, for all or for some. The one point is that mystical contemplation has no part in our present studies, and the tradition that restricts the use of the word contemplative to this one type must be rejected. In spite of support for this viewpoint in the tradition itself, good Christians still find the text-books terrifying. I am not interested in either supporting or denying the possibility of unmediated mystical ex-perience; it remains outside our premise. I live in this world and I believe in the creed, and neither my experience nor my belief knows anything of it. I side with Martin Buber (of whom more later): "I know nothing of a 'world' and a 'life in the world' that might separate a man from God. What is thus described is actually life with an alienated world of *It*, which experiences and uses. He who truly goes out to meet the world goes out also to God."[9]

I believe in God, Holy Trinity and Triune Being, and I believe that, on occasion, he has disclosed himself to me, but always through the beings and existents which participate in him because he lets them be. Such experience is contemplative in a com-bination of our first three uses of that term, not in the fourth sense about which I know nothing. I press the point only to substantiate my use of this word validly to describe a wide range of non-discursive prayer experience, and to assure my readers that they need not fear the text-books. Should any reader know first-hand of mysticism he has got hold of the wrong book.

Having said that, the text-books, especially in their anti-platonic stream, can still be of considerable help to us, especially when we are bold enough to use them critically. For our next task is to consider the preparatory steps necessary to the acquisition and development of a normal contemplative awareness of Triune Being, and thus to be prepared for his disclosure through the beings. This necessary preparation can again be summarised under four heads: *faith, morality, ascetic*, and *meditation*.

Faith is itself a unifying principle, since it recollects, in St. Teresa's sense, the scattered strands of existence. Faith demands commitment to a "master concern" to which all may be drawn,

9. *I and Thou* (Clark), p. 95.

and this is true on a psychological level where the concern is not necessarily overmastering. The dedicated craftsman, farmer or artist, even the responsible husband, are more integrated people — more "contemplative" — than play-boy, jack-of-all-trades, and dilettante. The former have a concern to which their energies are orientated, although contrary concerns may give rise to other tensions. It is only a "master concern" which is fully integrative, and this ultimately is faith in God, in Being.

> Authentic selfhood implies the attaining of a unified existence ... The conditions that this kind of unity may be brought into existence and authentic selfhood attained would seem to be that there should be both *commitment* and *acceptance*. Commitment is the prospective view of this unity, for it has to do with the future, with the possibilities of existence. A committed existence is one that has in view some master possibility. In consistently directing itself on this master possibility, the other possibilities of life are subordinated to it and the movement is towards unified selfhood ... But acceptance is just as necessary as commitment. Acceptance is the retrospective view of the self's unity, for it has to do with what has been, with the situation that already obtains and in which we find ourselves.[10]

That fits in well enough with traditional spirituality. St. François de Sales calls ordinary, or "acquired" contemplation, "the prayer of simple committal", where commitment to Christ is the "master concern". Acceptance is allied to penitence, an honest facing of the facts of the past together with acceptance of Christ's reconciliation. Acceptance is the core of the prayer of abandonment as taught by Bossuet and de Caussade, but this is enriched by the doctrine of infinite providential possibility, with its corollary decision-making, which in turn safeguards the prayer of abandonment from the errors of Quietism with which it is historically associated. This is but a contemporary, and non-mystical way of speaking of the divine obscurity and the divine darkness; the *via negativa* is largely concerned with the acceptance of God's provi-

10. *Principles of Christian Theology*, pp. 67–8.

dential awkwardness. So faith of this existential kind, not to be confused with intellectual belief, is the first step towards contemplative awareness of Being, since it is the prior unifying principle.

Hans von Balthasar says much the same thing:

> The act of contemplation, in which the believer hears the word of God and surrenders himself to it, is an act of the whole man. It cannot therefore assume a form in which man truncates his own being, whether for a short or longer time — for instance, by *systematically* training himself to turn from the outer world and attend wholly to the inner world, or turning from both the outer and inner senses (the imagination) to the pure, "naked" spirit. That kind of deliberate artificial restriction reduces man to a shadow of himself and is a misunderstanding of God's demand, namely "conversion", a turning from the manifold to the essential.[11]

We turn, secondly, to *morality* as preparatory to contemplation, and it is here that we meet the text-books at their most horrific. Sin is the fundamental disharmony, it is alienation, lostness, or concupiscence. Sin and contemplation — by whatever definition — are incompatible. But the unifying principle of acceptance includes penitence, and penitence forges forgiveness as the acceptance of Christ's reconciliation. To be forgiven means to overcome alienation which is the restoration of contemplative harmony, so if sin and forgiveness alternate throughout life — a regrettably yet indisputable fact — so also do the states of alienation and potential harmony, of lostness and contemplative awareness. To struggle after the contemplative awareness of triune Being, constantly to await the possibility of his disclosure, does not mean a once-for-all achievement, a sort of contemplative complacency, for that would be to deny everything we have said about existence as potentiality rather than as a status. This applies to faith itself, and is part of faith: "The man of faith, for his part, is not to be thought of as complacently anchored by his faith, for any faith

11. *Prayer*, p. 191.

worthy of the name will be subject to testing, and will not be a permanent possession but an attitude that has to be constantly renewed."[12]

This is what most of the text-books deny, for the only sort of contemplation they acknowledge is only entered into after interminable years of purgation — hardly the happiest word. The error, as von Balthasar points out,[13] is in treating the Three Ways as chronological stages in life's pilgrimage. First, purgation — for year after year — then contemplation of God unmediated: the old statue has at last been well and truly polished so that it can reflect the divine essence.

Nevertheless the moral struggle remains of the greatest importance, but here it is given a new slant and a new test. Pride, Anger, Lust, Sloth and Gluttony are unlikely to realise harmony within the self or society; Envy and Covetousness make little sense of loving cherry trees, of being at one with the created environment. None of these is compatible with sensing the disclosure of Being in the beings. The moral struggle remains as part, but only part, of choice which makes life.

The third necessary preparation for contemplative prayer is the *ascetic*; the traditional training of the spiritual athlete from I Corinthians 9: 24-7. Again the text-books veer towards the platonic, frightening the faithful and confusing the issue. Our present discussion revolves around two words: *mortification* and *detachment*.

The first comes from Colossians 3: 5, where St. Paul bids us to mortify, or kill, selfish desires, and from Galatians 2: 20; 5: 24, where he speaks of our being crucified with Christ. No one will quarrel with any of that: evil is to be attacked and killed; to be crucified with Christ is to be committed to him as our master concern, to share in his redemptive and reconciling cross. Sin means alienation, so the mortification of sin means the restoration of contemplative harmony. Sin is killed on the cross of Christ, and to be crucified with Christ means to be reconciled to, and to participate in, the sacred humanity: to become contemplatively aware of expressive Being manifested in the world. The Christian is bidden

12. *Principles of Christian Theology*, p. 71.
13. *Prayer*, p. 217.

"take up thy cross", and it has to be *thine*, so the text-books make the distinction between *necessary* and *voluntary* mortification.

The first is that commitment and acceptance which expresses faith, it is the acceptance of trials, misfortunes and sufferings creatively borne in the light of infinite providential possibility. It is free and faithful abandonment to God's awkwardness and Christ's unfairness. Voluntary mortification applies to those disciplines we take upon ourselves; fasting, the forgoing of legitimate pleasures and so on, and it is here that the platonic strand comes into its own, for in this context mortification means the suppression of the senses themselves. Practically all the classic writers warn against the unwholesome dangers inherent in this kind of thing, particularly in its exaggeration, yet few are prepared to eliminate it altogether. Few indeed are prepared to discount the mortification of the senses in favour of their positive nurture, yet this seems to be where our argument is leading.

We have been bold enough to suggest that if Christianity is the most materialistic of all religions then in existential terms it is also the most sensuous. This is now seen to enhance rather than detract from, the first, legitimate meaning of mortification. In a world beset by sin and suffering it is probable that misfortune, pain, sacrifice and penitence will play larger parts in the lives of serious Christians than will pleasures and joys. If we may truly speak of suffering, physical as well as mental and spiritual, as a genuine participation in Christ's passion, then sensuous pleasure, the taste of coffee and the warmth of the lover's embrace, must be an equally real participation in the incarnate life: being participates in Being, and more especially in the incarnation of expressive Being. If an ascetic of the platonic type so mortified his senses that he became oblivious of pain and wholly indifferent to mockings, scourgings and betrayal, it is difficult to see how he could really share in the passion of Christ. The glory and horror of the cross is not that Christ was mortified and indifferent but that he was infinitely sensitive. True ascetic suggests that the senses are to be not voluntarily mortified but heightened and nurtured.

To reject voluntary mortification of the senses is therefore to enhance the positive value of Christian *askesis*. A more authentic existence means greater, not less, sensitivity, and this still requires considerable discipline: the more you smoke the less you smell, the more you drink the less you taste. The old books place the gourmet and the glutton under the same head, yet the former could be the true ascetic. Anything that integrates, unifies, balances, simplifies and co-ordinates existence is preparation for contemplative experience, for an awareness of the disclosure of Being in the beings. It does not have to be "religious", and it need not be called anything so off-putting as voluntary mortification. The development of aesthetic appreciation, the co-ordinating skills of craftsmanship or even of games, the expending of loving care upon the material environment — home, garden and so on; all these things may be the ascetic preparation for a contemplative harmony in awareness of Triune Being. And this, be it remembered, is the point and purpose of it all.

It should now be clear what is wrong with "detachment". It is a negative idea which nevertheless warns against the root sin of idolatry. and it would be less confusing if all spiritual writers followed Macquarrie by saying so.[14] To be attached to creatures means to put them before God, to worship the beings instead of Being, but to be detached from creatures means little or nothing. It is reminiscent of the Prayer Book collect for Ash Wednesday, which cannot go so far as to state that God loves anything so compromises by saying that he hateth nothing. The confusion is brought out by the fact that nearly all the writers who use this idea immediately qualify it by some saving phrase. We are to be detached from creatures ... "except in so far" ... as they subserve the purposes of God, or help us towards our true end, or some such exception. But if we interpret this in existential-ontological language the exception becomes the positive rule: it is precisely what the creatures *must be made* to do. The confusion issues from the symbolic language of the old map, for here are three disparate facts: God made the world; it was very good; it fell. The new map expresses the same truths, but the picture looks different: Being lets-be the beings; creation, reconciliation and consummation are equiprimordial activities of Being; unitive Being strives continually to restore unity between the beings with Being. No being

14. *Principles of Christian Theology*, pp. 238–40.

can be detached from any other being or from Being, for all participate in Being and without the beings we can know nothing whatever of Being.

Meditation is the classic preparation for contemplative prayer, so we follow tradition in making it an important part of the phase I catechumenate. The distinction, however, is that if contemplation is interpreted in our elementary, non-mystical way, it follows upon mental prayer naturally and immediately. According to the mystical tradition, the two are separated by thirty years, if contemplation ever arrives at all. We confront the old error of a chronological understanding of the Three Ways.

Our -ontological foundation, the creed, is ultimately a whole; not only the Trinity but all Christian doctrine fuses into a single revelation. The creed must indeed be understood, grasped, and this necessitates analysis and discursive examination. But the end-product of all theology is truth contemplated; seen and admired at a single glance. This is only to apply a spiritual principle to intellectual understanding; that contemplative rest is the proper end and consummation of all activity. It was so with God on the seventh day of creation, it was so with Christ in the tomb on Holy Saturday — the "greater Sabbath" — it was so with our man in his garden, and it is the same with theological truth. Cardinal Lecaro puts this well: "It is, indeed, quite natural that once the human mind has gained possession of the truth after much labour in reasoning and analysis, it should rest in the calmer activity of synthesis, of admiration, and, as it were, of savouring."[15] So does Tanquery:

Later on another simplification is effected: the short space of time given to reflection is replaced by an *intuitive intellectual gaze*. We thereby come to understand first principles without effort, as by an intuition. After we have meditated for a long time upon the fundamental truths of the spiritual life, they become to us as certain and clear as first principles, and at one glance we grasp them with ease and delight, without recourse to a detailed analysis.[16]

15. *Methods of Mental Prayer* (Burns, Oates), p. 250.
16. *The Spiritual Life*, n. 1366, pp. 638–9.

This process is speeded up not only by our particular — "lower" — interpretation of contemplation, but also by the introduction of existential-ontological language. One reason why meditation has played so large a part in traditional spirituality is that the substantive language of its credal formulae asks for this kind of treatment. It is difficult to *contemplate* the trinity of Father, Son and Holy Ghost; it is equally difficult to *meditate* on triune Being: the first demands to be understood, the second to be grasped. Our catechumenate phase follows tradition in seeing discursive reflection as prologue to the contemplation of truth. It rejects tradition in seeing it as but a tentative preliminary for most Christians.

THIRTEEN

The Prayer of Empathy

ANY ATTEMPT to formulate a contemporary spirituality runs into a linguistic dilemma. Classical terminology is notoriously ambiguous yet the key words are so embedded in history and tradition that one hesitates to change them. A new word can be as confusing as a carefully defined old one, despite its subtle nuances. Such a word is contemplation; in one sense a common word yet in this context so loaded in favour of non-sensory platonic mysticism that we are tempted to search for another. If our stress is to be on harmony, integration, love for creation, thence the disclosure of Being through the beings, such a new term might be *empathetic* prayer. The Oxford Dictionary defines empathy as "the power of projecting one's personality into (and so fully comprehending) the object of contemplation". In the context of Christian prayer, "fully to comprehend" can mean no less than to see into the reality of something as a being let-be by Being. This in turn means to love, to see a being as focus of the Trinity and that which discloses the Trinity.

How does one learn to practise prayer of this kind? Having made the necessary preparations, as described in the preceding chapter, and having seen that these preparations tend to fuse into the prayer itself instead of being mere prolegomena, what do I do next?

Interpreting doctrine according to the new map, which is contemplative, or synthetic, rather than discursive, we may well begin with the liturgy. Traditionally the divine office is offered in objective, volitional, non-discursive praise to God the Father; such prayer can properly be made only "in the Spirit" and "through Jesus Christ Our Lord". But the stress is on the transcendence of God, and to keep the mind thus firmly fixed on God, as to refuse to be drawn into subjective and discursive cogitations, is itself a contemplative technique. It is re-collective, a gathering together of one's whole being which is drawn towards a single point. Such worship is a traditional ideal, but it is very difficult with anything as complex as the Prayer Book office in the setting of the substantive formula of the Trinity. If we begin not with Father, Son and Spirit but with a sinking into triune Being, things are enormously simplified. Transcendent (or primordial) Being is unitive Being immanent in me, striving to unite my being with Being itself; Being is manifested, outpoured, expressed in me by expressive Being. I sink into Being and triune Being takes me over; the Blessed Trinity dwells in my heart if you want to put it that way. And the words of the office flow out, unitive Being speaks them, pushes them out in divine striving to Being I can now call Father; expressive Being takes the words and redeems them, and my praise is transcendental. My praise, my offering, my sacrifice and oblation do not go "out" or "up" or "through" or "away" because all is offered to God who is not "out or "up' or "through" or "away". God just *is*, and if we can possibly say that he *is* anything else then we can only say that he is triune.

Such prayer is contemplative in type since it is neither discursive nor meditative. But it is impossible if its liturgical vehicle is a lengthy structure interspersed with psalms and collects you have to find in a book and lessons you have to seek in a lectionary and then look up in a Bible. By contrast, the proposed eucharistic-prologue-office is admirable for the purpose. It is not too difficult to achieve as concentrate of life, which will then rebound on life itself as a harmonising and integrating influence.

The eucharist is both concentrate of life and concentrate of Christian doctrine: a creed in action. It forms part of our phase I catechumenate, since it is to be dissected, meditated upon, learned and understood. But ultimately, and reasonably soon, it may be subjected to the same technique. There is one simple rule: sink into Being and throw away the books.

The next and more personal stage may best be discussed by borrowing the concepts of the *mantra* and *mandala* from oriental religion. The first is a short devotional phrase, to be repeated over and over again until its significance sinks into the consciousness and indeed sub-consciousness. Its significance is to be contemplatively absorbed, inwardly digested, entered into empathetically. Such technique is common in the tradition of Western Christianity, with Hugh of St. Victor, St. François de Sales, St. Ignatius Loyola, John de Fécamp, Augustine Baker and Julian of Norwich, as possibly its best known exponents. But the most obvious Christian example is the "Jesus Prayer" of Eastern Orthodoxy. This classic of devotional-contemplative phrases runs: "Lord Jesus Christ, Son of God, have mercy on me, a sinner." It is significant that Western *mantras* are generally shorter than this venerable formula which still looks like a discursive series of facts for meditation. It is therefore a common practice to reduce it to the single word "Jesus".

A *mandala* ("circle" in Sanskrit) is a visual symbol for some ultimate truth. In the East it is usually circular, often elaborated, as symbol of the One, the undifferentiated Godhead. The star of David and the Cross are other examples: symbols to be contemplated not discussed, absorbed not understood. The idea is common enough in Christian devotion: the crucifix and icon, statuettes and holy pictures, are all foci for the attention and concentration of those engaged in the prayer of simplicity. But to many today this sort of thing is tinged with artificiality, it appears to be (though of course need not necessarily be) suggestive of that anti-worldly pietism we are trying to avoid. I therefore make the suggestion that, in the light of our new doctrinal map, the significant *mandala* is that being which happens to disclose Being, be it cherry tree, steel pylon or dingy cattle shed. If we are to borrow the symbolism of the oriental circle, it is hard to do better than a daisy. Dare I suggest that the most apposite modern *mantra* is "Being lets-be"? Or "Being-Being-Being", or if you like, and it comes to the same doctrinal thing, "Being-Jesus". This could be the beginning of contemplative awareness as an habitual stake, the beginning of life in triune Being.

The technique of *mandala* traditionally depends on sight, because sight is the one sense from which even Puritan and Manichee cannot wholly escape. But we welcome the sensory as sanctified in the incarnation, as experience of the sacred humanity. So what of the others, especially touch and smell? The idea is not so unorthodox as might at first appear. The Rosary depends upon the recollective value of touch, and the Church has a place for incense. But both of these suffer from opposite yet common defects in our Western tradition; the first is too complex, the second is too pious. Through the incarnation any being can disclose Being by any or all of the senses; the feel of warm metal, held lovingly in the hands, the texture of wood or stone, can be of recollective, integrative value when totally attended to. So of course can pain, suffering, toothache, which is the point already made: if we can truly enter into the sufferings of Christ through our own, it is but logical that he can truly share our sensory joys and manifest his presence through them. But for present purposes, concerned as we are with recollective or empathetic prayer, it is probably the simpler sensations, the feel of the beads of the Rosary, which assist us most. But the Rosary prayer is too complex to be anything but meditative or discursive; we need no prayers, no formulae, only our *mantra* and *mandala*: Being lets-be, Being-Christ: warm lead and the taste of coffee.

So with smell, but it need not be anything as ecclesiastical as incense: roses, lavender, soap or shoe polish do just as well. The need is to re-collect one's total being through concentration on a single point, for this is response to Being's self-disclosure, acceptance of prayer as relation.

However, contemplative awareness, the recollected prayer of empathy is to be carried out in the world. The foregoing methods, or techniques, or whatever we call them, might help towards this but they are only preparatory. There remains the doctrine of divine prevenience, God acts first, God holds the initiative, God cannot be sought or found, or even lost, by our own efforts. Prayer is relation forged by God himself, that is why it must be permanent and continuous. Our part is response. But God manifests himself through the beings; we first become aware of the divine presence in the world, through creation and through the senses. How do we respond?

The greatest assistance I have discovered is in the renowned work of Martin Buber, significantly Jewish yet so easily Christianised because it is basically trinitarian. Buber's *I and Thou* has been subjected to commentary after commentary, speculation

L

after speculation; all we can add is something about the relation between this famous thesis and the existential-ontological approach of Macquarrie.

In the first place Buber is strongly and strangely anti-platonic:

> To look away from the world, or to stare at it, does not help a man to reach God ... Men do not find God if they stay in the world. They do not find Him if they leave the world. He who goes out with his whole being to meet his *Thou* and carries to it all being that is in the world, finds Him who cannot be sought.
>
> Of course God is the "wholly Other"; but He is also the wholly Same, the wholly Present. Of course He is the *Mysterium Tremendum* that appears and overthrows; but He is also the mystery of the self-evident, nearer to me than my *I*.
>
> If you explore the life of things and of conditioned being you come to the unfathomable, if you deny the life of things and of conditioned being you stand before nothingness, if you hallow this life you meet the living God.[1]

There are two ways of looking at things, at the beings, at the world. The first is the way of objectivity, or of meditation, of discursiveness, of scientific analysis, or indeed of exploitation, and it is signified by the relation *I-It*. The second is the way of contemplation, of empathy, of fusion, harmony, humility and love, which is the relation of *I-Thou*. The latter is the ultimate existential relation, concerning one's total being; the former cannot so be, for it involves a disintegration, a loss or lack of existence, an unfulfilled potential. In an *I-Thou* relation the reality is neither *I* nor *Thou* but the relation, it implies a fusion, a harmony, a loving. And this is what I mean by prayer as relation, not as act, or devotional experience, or words or formulae or method. In practice, prayer will contain some of these "experiences" (a word Buber uses in an ambiguous and derogatory sense implying *I-It*) but these experiences, or feelings, or even "answers" are not

1. *I and Thou*, p. 79.

prayer: prayer is relation, or as Buber puts it: "All real living is meeting."[2]

> To this end the world of sense does not have to be laid aside as though it were illusory. There is no illusory world, there is only the world — which appears to us as two-fold in accordance with our two-fold attitude. Only the barrier of separation has to be destroyed. Further, no "going beyond sense-experience" is necessary; for every experience, even the most spiritual, could yield us only an *It*.[3]

> In every sphere in its own way, through which process of becoming that is present to us we look out towards the fringe of the eternal *Thou*; in each we are aware of a breath from the eternal *Thou*; in each *Thou* we address the eternal *Thou* . . . I CONSIDER A TREE . . .[4]

This is the crux. I CONSIDER A TREE. The tree is my *mandala*, Hugh of St. Victor's "symbol", Julian of Norwich's hazelnut; to Macquarrie a being let-be by Being. But I too am a being let-be by Being, so I do not have to forge, or enter into, a relation with the tree: I have to recognise, accept, submit to, a relation that is already there. I do not have to go out to meet the tree but to sink into Being, for in Being we are met, and we might meet Being.

There can be no "method" yet there remains the struggle for self-discipline, the positive *askesis*. I go out to the tree as a being participating in Being, I exist because of Being's expressive outpouring, so does the tree. I contemplate it, gaze upon it in admiration, empathetically, unwaveringly, and for a long time; I love it and become one with it and if need be I can feel it, embrace it, smell it, repeating my *mantra*: Being lets-be. I am in harmony with the tree, and through it with creation, perhaps with Being, but I have not forged the relation. That is the work of unitive Being, so I submit, yield, give-in; or if you wish, surrender to the Holy Ghost.

2. *I and Thou*, p. 11.
3. *I and Thou*, p. 77.
4. *I and Thou*, pp. 6–7.

A *mantra*, however simple, and because of its recollective power of simplifying, presupposes some previous understanding, some study and meditation, absorbed into oneself. A *mantra* is a contemplative simplification of truth which has been analysed. I now know that Being lets-be is, as it were, short for primordial Being is outpoured in risk through expressive Being who became incarnate in Jesus Christ and redeemed all the beings; unitive Being is now at this present existential moment, striving to reunite in harmony all the beings with Being; Being goes on creating, reconciling, consummating, and all is focused on my relation with the tree; with meeting, with relation. This is prayer, because in Buber's words I am looking towards the fringe, placing myself in a possible awareness of Being's disclosure; I am responding to the address of the eternal Thou.

This is only the beginning. *I-Thou* and *I-It* alternate, for to remain in the former state would be complete sanctity. But I hope that this prayer, this concentrate of what life is glimpsed to be, this empathetic harmony, will lead into a habit, not of permanent *I-Thou* relationships, but a habit of interpreting the whole of life, *I-It* phases as well, in terms of God who is revealed as one Holy and undivided Trinity. It is not far from Julian of Norwich's hazel nut, for she knew that "it is all that is made", for "God made it . . . God loveth it . . . God keepeth it".[5] "And after this I saw God in a Point, that is to say, in mine understanding — by which sight I saw that He is in all things."[6] And "the Blissful Trinity, our maker, in Christ Jesus our Saviour, endlessly dwelleth in our soul, worshipfully ruling and protecting all things . . ."[7] The only difference is the terminology: perhaps "God is Trinity", or "God above, around, within", of "Father-Son-Spirit", or "Jesus", are better examples of the Christian *mantra*, but to me they do not quite come off: *de gustibus non disputandum est!*

Buber follows his approach to the tree with confrontation with a human being[8] just as we have done in our movement from the

5. *Revelations*, 1, 5.
6. *Revelations*, III, 11.
7. *Revelations*, Preface, 1.
8. *I and Thou*, pp. 8–9.

disclosure of Holy Being in nature to an awareness of Christ in others.[9] One can barely contemplate a person — it would not be very polite — but the empathetic contemplation of things leads into the personal *I-Thou* relation of love. In life we are forced to analyse, pastors especially have to pull people apart, clarify their sins and minister to their discovered weaknesses and graces. But the principle of rest — *anapauo* — remains the final consummation, even in the confessional. As God rested, in loving contemplation, on the seventh day of creation, so our gardener completed his mowing and weeding by restful empathy. So also does any worthy work of pastoral ministration, it is completed by love, by the contemplation, and admiration, of the whole integrated person. That, too, is Christ in others.

E. L. Mascall has been bold enough to call activity, mere activity, diabolical, for it is the essential characteristic of the devil, "because your adversary the devil, as a roaring lion, walketh about, seeking whom he may devour . . ."[10] He is not hungry, he has no need to devour anyone, it is activity which is absolutely purposeless and unredeemed, for "The purpose of activity is rest."[11] Theology, our Phase I catechumenate, is by nature analytic and discursive, and it too can be diabolical if it does not find rest in contemplation. So it is with the pastoral dissection of human beings, the end product must be love which is what our search for Christ in other people is all about. Perhaps we should coin another phrase, psycho-synthesis as complement and consummation of psycho-analysis? Perhaps we should teach contemplative penitence as the final stage of a detailed examination of conscience?

In devotional tradition God *rested* on the seventh day, actively and lovingly contemplating his finished creation, and it is this love which keeps all things in being. The Sabbath rest was both end and beginning, the consummation of the original creation and the beginning of that continuous creative activity by which the world subsists. So the cross is both end and beginning of reconciliation, the final victory and the initiation of the eschatological end, with

9. *See* Chapters 7, 8 above.
10. 1 Peter 5: 8.
11. *Grace and Glory* (Faith Press, 1961), p. 24.

the tomb — Holy Saturday — as watershed between the two eras. It is easy to see what is wrong with this old picture; three successive stages instead of one activity of a triune God. Apart from that, God's love "pouring down" on to creation is a difficult concept if we are to be aware of the divine presence manifested in the beings. God lets-be, Being lets-be, makes better sense, not only as theological explanation but as empathetic prayer. The old map only says God loves; the new map says God is Loving, which is much the same as saying God rests.

Sane experiment must continue. Having thrown off the more fearsome elements of platonic mysticism, many sources open up before us. Suffice it to mention the findings of contemporary psychology, especially those that speak of "self-actualisation" and of the "development of potential". This kind of thing could easily become stunted and stuntish, but married to theology it can add greatly to techniques, if so they may be called, of contemplative awareness.

We have borrowed sparingly from the Orient, and again a fruitful source of research and experiment opens up, especially if we take to heart what Macquarrie says about Christianity in relation to other religions.[12] Zen and Yoga might help us towards integrated harmony, the first step towards the contemplative, and breathing exercises have played a small part within the Christian tradition. To call the third person of the holy Trinity the breath of God is dangerous, to link this with human breath could be disastrous. But deep-breathing exercises are integrative, and if Being lets-be, then breath as the symbol of the striving of unitive Being is not so far-fetched.

There remains a further factor in the development of a contemplative outlook, the supreme environment of creativity, and perhaps the most real of all foci or concentrates of life. To coin a phrase: the *rest* is *silence*.

12. *Principles of Christian Theology*, pp. 134–58.

FOURTEEN

Silence

CONTEMPORARY SPIRITUALITY is suspicious of "with-drawal" into acts of prayer, and the modern world is frightened of that silence which goes with it. This is understandable, even laudable, if it is an attack of religiosity, a rebellion against pushing God out on to the perimeter of life. But we have forestalled this interpretation by reversing the process-product relation of the old *regula*: acts of prayer are not so much framework and preparation for life as life itself in concentrated form. Periodic acts of prayer do not sanctify life since life is in God, and therefore sanctified already; prayer underlines and articulates the fact. Withdrawal into silence is no escape but a concentrated confrontation with reality. Nevertheless the process-product relation, whichever way round we put it, is reciprocal; the disciplined use of silence is one of the traditional means towards contemplation and its value cannot be gainsaid. But we speak of contemplation as, primarily, guide to life and decision in triune Being, not as an accomplishment in its own right.

If withdrawal into silence is focus or concentrate of experience, then it is a necessary and natural need, not an artificially imposed religious duty. Silence is the environment of creativity, the essential condition for letting-be, the birthplace of love. One does not usually compose poetry on Paddington station in the rush hour, although such experience may well provide the initial inspiration for a poem. Sleep and waking, incubation and birth, winter and summer, rest and action, habitual awareness of Being and acts of penitence and praise: this is the natural order of things. Those who run from silence are the real escapists for they dare not confront reality.

It is common experience to ordinary Christians in retreat, or after a prolonged period of silent prayer, for things, beings, creation, to take on a new and more vivid appearance. The cultivation of a deep interior silence issues in a new look towards everything, the presence and manifestation of Being in the beings is constant, but here is a positive response to that constancy. Under such conditions Julian contemplated her hazel nut; to George Fox things had "another smell than before"; St. Francis called wind and water brother and sister, not out of sentiment, but as a theological expression of contemplation; to John Scotus Erigena the world became "a theophany". In Buber's terminology they had all moved into an *I-Thou* relationship. In Macquarrie's, human being became united with other beings and glimpsed Being. In all cases it is prayer, emphatic and contemplative.

We have spoken of the cultivation of a deep interior silence, but that is misleading, for silence, like contemplation, ultimately precludes method and technique; one can only understand, experiment, and risk. Silence is positive, it is not the absence of noise, for in any case there is no such thing in nature as noiselessness. It has to be deep and interior, and it may be achieved against a background of din, for the sense of hearing follows the same pattern as the other senses. The constant, pin-pointed gaze at the *mandala* — or tree or pylon or daisy — the constant touch of the Rosary bead, the enveloping smell of incense or soap; all these may integrate and concentrate. So may a constant background drone. But if this interior quiet, which is active response to the disclosure of Being, cannot be induced by method, it can be experimented with, and it is of assistance if the process is psychologically and theologically understood.

The word *anapauo* — I rest — is fundamental to the biblical understanding of contemplation. We must now introduce another biblical word as the typological foundation of withdrawal into silence: the word is *eremos* — desert, lonely place, devastated country, or more commonly, wilderness. This word has a wide variety of meanings which for present purposes may be considered under three headings.

First, it applies to a wilderness or desert as the scene of danger and desolation. It is the haunt of the Gadarene Demoniac in Luke

8: 29. It is a place of physical peril for St. Paul[1] and for the multi-
tude of the faithful.[2] It may also mean a city or country
devastated by enemy action: "And Jesus knew their thoughts and
said unto them, every kingdom divided against itself is brought to
desolation (*eremoutai*)."[3] Or it can be a place abandoned by its
inhabitants, "Behold your house is left unto you desolate."[4] In
Matthew 12: 43, both key words are found in conjunction:
"When the unclean spirit is gone out of man, he walketh through
dry places seeking rest (*anapausin* — resting place) and findeth
none."

It is not difficult to translate this into spiritual-theology. From
danger of demons and wild beasts to spiritual danger is a short
step, desolation is the opposite of consolation, and perhaps it is not
too far-fetched to see dry-places as the outcome of desolation,
dryness or aridity of spirit.

Secondly, the word also carries the opposite connotation of
safety and, again, rest. It is the refuge of the persecuted, as in
I Kings, 19, where Elijah flees from Jezebel into the wilderness,
there to find rest and spiritual refreshment typified by the miraculous cake and cruse of water. But, looking back to our first
heading, Elijah first gives up hope and prays for death; looking
forward to our third heading, it is here that ultimately God
appears, or if you wish Being is disclosed in the still small voice. To
our Lord the wilderness is a special place of communion with the
Father: "And in the morning, rising up a great while before day,
he went out and departed into a solitary place, and there
prayed."[5] It is also a direct instruction to the disciples: "And he
said unto them, come ye yourselves apart into a desert place, and
rest a while."[6] Again *eremos* and *anapauo* in conjunction.

The third meaning is a synthesis of the preceding two, in that it
emphasises the aspect of fruitfulness, creativity, and victory. In the
stories of Moses and Elijah the result is prophetic insight, divine

1. 2 Corinthians 11: 26.
2. Hebrews 11: 38.
3. Matthew 12: 25.
4. Matthew 23: 38; Luke 13: 35; Acts 1: 20.
5. Mark 1: 35; cf. Matthew 14: 13; Luke 4: 42; John 11: 54.
6. Mark 6: 31.

disclosure, and the retreat into the silent desert brings Jesus victory. How important, and how significant, are things, beings, physical manifestation, in these desert stories: the manna,[7] the water from the rock, the bitter water made sweet,[8] Elijah's mantle,[9] and so on. Later the wilderness becomes the expected scene of Messiah's advent. John the Baptist comes out of the wilderness with the greatest prophetic message ever. *Eremos* takes on an eschatological significance for it is out of the desert that Christ will return in glory, finally to vanquish the powers of darkness. It is in the wilderness that the Church should remain when the terrible signs of the end appear and here the community of faith are to live, listening in silence for the disclosure of the silent God.

That is very sketchy and no doubt the biblical scholars could produce minutely documented tomes on the significance of these two words alone. Here it suffices to note the curiously constant progression: fear and danger, followed by rest and safety, followed by creativity, prophecy and victory. Not infrequently the order follows in the same story: Elijah wants to die in despair, then refreshment, then the disclosure of the still small voice. Out of Egypt into the wilderness is the beginning of Jewish religious consciousness. But the Exodus led to heartsearching, temptation, desolation and sin. Yet hope remained, and through the silent wilderness was the way to that good land, flowing with milk and honey. If we take our typology seriously, Isaiah's great hymn to silence remains very pertinent indeed: "The wilderness and the solitary place shall be glad for them; and the desert shall rejoice and blossom as the rose. It shall blossom abundantly, and rejoice even with joy and singing: the glory of Lebanon shall be given unto it, the excellency of Carmel and Sharon, they shall see the glory of the Lord, and the excellency of our God."[10] I do not quote that because it sounds nice, or in case the reader has not heard it before, but because it takes on a new twist: out of silence shall come fragrance, even the trees shall manifest God's presence.

7. Exodus 16: 14 ff.
8. Exodus 15: 25.
9. 2 Kings 2: 8.
10. Isaiah 35: 1–2.

The supreme exemplar is Christ himself. Gethsemane starts with tears and fear and bloody sweat, then the peace of God, then the victory: "thy will be done". So with the temptation narrative: the long frightening vigil, the battle, the victory.

What does this mean? Neither silence nor contemplation are reducible to method but here is understanding of what might be expected if the experiment is risked. Suppose a man, a modern man brings a period of silence into his weekly scheme of prayer, an hour, preferably three hours, as concentrate of the experience of Being in daily life. What is he expected to do? And what might he expect to happen? I cannot answer the first question, for there is no method: I can only say sink into Being, relax, recollect, look, feel. The answer to the second question is easier. The desert of silence will at first be frightening and dangerous, and considerable tensions will develop. Everything seems strange and artificial, and of special consequence to modern Christians there may be a sense of false piety, of religiosity. In spite of everything previously explained, here I am devoutly saying my prayers in apparent isolation from the world. It is all very uncomfortable. But the Bible has explained this as normal, as the proper start of the creative prayer of silence: it is Elijah giving up and petitioning for death; Christ sweating blood in Gethsemane. It is all part of the game.

There is also likely to be temptation of a particularly virulent kind. The desert as traditional haunt of the demons is full of existential meaning. It was not by accident that our Lord suffered temptation after a silent and solitary sojourn in the wilderness: it was why he went there, being "led up of the spirit".[11] And it was this example which was followed in the experiments of the Desert Fathers. The flight to the desert was no negative rejection of the world but a positive search for God, but it was first a positive search for the devil. It was assumed, with curious optimism, that Satan had been driven out of the cities, to be persuaded into the desert for a final mopping-up operation. It was as purposeful as Christ's self initiated temptation and victory, and it is unlikely that St. Anthony and St. Jerome were surprised to find themselves assailed by carnal temptations. They knew what they were doing and courageously sallied forth to battle.

11. Matthew 4: 1; Luke 4: 1.

This discomfiture, awkwardness, and temptation can last a long time, and it is obviously a concentrate of a common state of life; a fight against alienation and disharmony which in the busy world easily gets shrugged off and left to fester. With perseverance it will pass into the second stage of rest, peace, contentment and contemplation. This is a concentrate of life in its better moods, and this stage can also last a long time.

The third stage is victory, inspiration, prophecy and discernment, but this, like God himself, cannot be sought. We can only respond to the divine omni-presence and omni-activity, omni-active-contemplation, or in less clumsy terms, to God's continuous letting-be. This third stage is likely to be carried back into everyday living, it is the seed-bed of that discernment which is the third aspect of decision-making. Like sacramental grace, discernment does not come to us in semi-Pelagian doses, it gradually develops with our response to being let-be.

Nevertheless, after a prolonged period of silence the world looks different, things appear in sharper reality, and Being may be disclosed in them.

This kind of prayer is under attack from three quarters and some defence should be offered. First, the text-book, which frequently places it under the third of the falsely chronological Three Ways. In order to attempt such contemplation in silence one must first be half-way, or perhaps nine-tenths of the way, to heaven. Here the object of contemplation is God in himself, not Being in the beings; a confusion with which we have dealt. And we have seen with crystal clarity from the Bible that this retreat into the desert, rather than being only possible after the defeat of sin, is in fact the battle itself. There is a strong case for the view that it is the sinner not the saint for whom such prayer is meant, yet in the text-books it is the sinner who is precluded from attempting it.

It is attacked by the modern radical, who sees this prayer as the epitome of self-centred pietism, as escape into religiosity. This criticism is overcome by our basic thesis that all prayer is relation and that acts of prayer are foci of life itself. We have also seen that false piety, like sin itself, is overcome as we persevere from the first stage into the second. In the modern world the escape from reality

is not into the desert but into the crowd; not into silence but into
the din.

Silent prayer demands long periods of time and serious Christians look upon it as too difficult for them. This stems from the
text-book approach with its Three Ways confusion and its
platonic-mystical slant. It is demonstrated as false by the remarkable record of the Retreat Movement. Year by year many
thousands of people, schoolgirls, undergraduates and professional
men amongst them, not only manage to survive a three days'
retreat in silence, but discover a new medium of creativity. Their
eyes and ears are opened to the disclosure of Being.

The principle of the annual retreat, however, suffers certain
disadvantages when it is placed within our new-map framework.
Prayer is life in concentrate, and one must question the feasibility
of a three-day concentrate of twelve months. What we are ad-
vocating is more like a weekly, or monthly "quiet day". The
trouble with the conventional quiet day is that it is not very quiet,
being generally prostituted by services and addresses. A quiet day,
moreover, is notoriously difficult to manage infrequently, and it is
well known that, to the beginner, a full three-day retreat is very
much easier to cope with. Retreat, therefore, might well play its
part within the phase one catechumenate stage, leaving the solitary quiet day, or quiet few hours, is the normal practice in
proficient Christian living. But it would have to be fairly frequent.
That is by the way; we are concerned with principles not rules.
We are still building upon our premise: I live in this world and I
believe in the creed; what do I do next? From this existential-
ontological basis, from living experience in the world, from Christian discipleship, from the fundamental religious experience of
awareness of Being in the beings; from all this the need for silence
has arisen. 'Be still, and know that I am God"[12] is no pious ex-
hortation but a pastoral-theological fact.

12. Psalm 46: 10.

FIFTEEN

Personal Conclusion

AUTHORS ARE sometimes invited to write the dust-jacket blurb
for their own book, which gives them the not very wholesome
opportunity to tell the world what a wonderful book they have
written. It would be more appropriate if they were asked, in
honest and sincere Christian humility, to *review* their own books.
The author, more than anyone, ought to be able to explain what
his book is about, and that is the primary object of a review.
Secondly, the author, if he claims the humble minimum, knows
better than anyone else where his book has failed. How many
writers have writhed under the lash of the inconsequent reviewer
who has simply missed the point? How many writers have enjoyed
the fourth martini with their friends because the professional reviewer has failed to spot the one significant weakness in the argument?

I began this book with an apologetic for the personal. I end it
with a personal appraisal; my own notes for a self-imposed
review.

Dr. Macquarrie manages to be contemporary without undue
strain. He writes as a scholar for scholars without affectation. The
pastoral-theologian is in a different position, he must get the message across in living language to his fellow Christians. Where might
I have failed?

Theology must be contemporary, it must speak to the world in
the existential present tense, or it is not theology, which freely
translated means the living Word of God. But there is no point or
purpose in being fashionable, in being in the vogue, because theology, however it changes, is concerned with eternal values;
fashion is by definition passing and superficial. Nothing is gained

by changing words: this is one of my personal difficulties with Dr. Macquarrie's distinguished predecessor Paul Tillich. He changed words, but to say that "sin" is meaningless to the modern generation so let us call it "alienation" instead does not really solve anything. You cannot understand "alienation" unless you first understand "sin". But as a personal judgment, Macquarrie has done much more than this; by changing words he has changed prayer, by reinterpretation of the creed he has charged the revelation with new life.

If I walk across Piccadilly Circus, or look across Times Square, or stand in the Place de la Concorde, and think that God the Almighty Father, having rested on the seventh day, still continues lovingly to grant value to it all; that everything is there because of his loving contemplation of it, then all I am conscious of is trying to be religious. If I transfer the scene to the New Forest or the Alleghany mountains it does not make any difference, except that there I can be religious without getting run down. But if I say Being lets-be I am not just changing the words, I am changing the whole scheme of things and bringing it to life. God is. And he is active, making the wheels go round, striving to reunite everything into a theophany, and I am in something like a contemplative state.

If I walk along saying "Jesus", or "Christ is with me", then it is either a theological fact of faith or a phoney religious emotion; it does not ring true. If I say Being lets-be then Christ *is* present, simply and naturally. If I think about my sins, and Christ's redeeming Passion, if I meditate about the cross, then again I am either thinking theology or vainly striving after an affective devotion which is foreign. If I am all at sea with my thoughts and emotions, lost and out of harmony with things and I say Being lets-be, then I am penitent: I want to go to confession, not because it is the rule but because it is necessary. I am devoted to Julian of Norwich, and I have made a deep study of Margery Kempe, but I do not claim their affective gifts. A child in pain affects me far more than the thought of Christ on the cross, so I look for a connection, and find it in the incarnation of expressive Being; not deeply in the dark night but in the sensual clarity of broad daylight. Perhaps this is what Fr. Geoffrey Curtis means when he says that "The whole concept of contemplation is still in need of being fully *incarnationalised*".[1]

In spite of support from eminent scholars, I foresee the charge of arrogance in rejecting so much of traditional mystical theology. I am not refuting it: in my experience, the first part of my premise, I know nothing at all about it, and I do not believe that such experience is necessary to salvation. Coupled with this accusation will be that of a sort of Chestertonian optimism; most of my examples and illustrations are either happy or trivial ones. What has happened to the cross, to the essential toughness and asceticism of genuine discipleship? Is not everything in the garden rather too lovely? What of the intractable tragedies of the modern world; racism, the ghetto, poverty, starvation, violence and degradation? Such criticism is more difficult to combat; I can only plead that genuine new ways of prayer, compatible with the contemporary outlook, are not disconnected with the totality of the Church's mission. When I speak, possibly too often, of integration, contemplative harmony, and so on, I hope that this will not be misconstrued as merely psychological, as comfort masquerading as prayer. It is still only the beginning of a disciplined response to grace, and I think it is a more realistic one than toddling off to church on Sunday and feeling good about it. Pastorally, I am concerned to be of some service, by the grace of God, to those modern Christians who do precisely this yet feel frustrated. This is my excuse for the optimism, and for the rejection of platonic-mysticism — the text-book approach. The committed Christian banker, the concerned typist, the happy farmer of faith and the devout bricklayer; these are the most neglected people in the Western Church today. Their situation, their environment, their *facticity*, is incompatible with a good deal of traditional teaching. I should like to help them to be different from the mystical-textbook disciple without feeling guilty or inferior. Commitment and martyrdom may coincide, or they may not, but the hair shirt under the ermine strikes me as being a little out of date: as a compromise it is not even honest. The positive and purposeful development of the senses demands every bit as much discipline as their suppression.

1. *Christian Spirituality Today*, ed. G.A.M. Ramsey (Faith Press, 1961), p. 59.

One further difficulty, a further criticism — though there will doubtless be many more — is that of evasion. Have I exaggerated the theological interest of my banker, typist, farmer and bricklayer? The strong point about the old *regula* is that it told you what to do without a lot of theologising, it appealed to the unlettered, which is not the same as the illiterate and certainly not the same as the unintelligent. In tradition the unlettered are those of the faithful who know no Latin and who are not interested in theology. In spite of the revival of interest, are not the majority of the faithful still in this classic category? It could be so, but I remain doubtful whether *Christian Proficiency* still meets the need.

Put to the pastoral test, moreover, this criticism could rebound upon itself. Granted a growing minority of the theologically interested, what is the status of the rest? For there are still a great many committed Christians around the Western world, how thinly spread is of little consequence. Convention, puerile fear, and other such unworthy motives may still account for a certain amount of Christian practice, in the superficial sense, but I am sure that this would also involve a minority. It leaves us with those whose faith is genuine, doctrinally sound, but inarticulate, uncritical, and unlettered. Such faith is not discursively thought out, not subjected to critical analysis, so it must be contemplative in the non-platonic, non-mystical sense we have tried to describe: there is no other category into which it can be fitted. Over the years the old familiar phrases have floated around these faithful ears, Father, Son and Holy Ghost; persons, natures and substances; suffered under Pontius Pilate, sitteth on the right hand of God; until the underlying truths have been absorbed, their significance has been grasped. This could prove the normality of the contemplative. I have no wish radically to change it all for fashion's sake, yet in the hands of faithful pastors perhaps the process towards spiritual maturity could be speeded, and eased, by reference to the new map. Last-ditch apologetic might be replaced by exciting and practical Christian adventure.

Pastoral-theology is a link in a chain; in the last resort every pastor, clerical or lay, and ultimately every individual Christian, has to make his own adaptation of doctrine, and his own personal decision. I can only hope that, in conjunction with

M

others, these speculations and suggestions will link up somewhere.

As critique and perhaps sequel to *Christian Proficiency*, this book has been written from an Anglican viewpoint, since any such study has to be written from some viewpoint. In opposition to a certain fashionable opinion I do not believe there is such a thing as a pure, overall Christian spirituality, since such would have to discount particular tradition and culture which are formative factors in any theology. Nevertheless, the tentative conclusions I have reached, and many of the suggestions I have made, have much ecumenical significance.

The type of contemplative and empathetic prayer I have tried to expound — a trinitarian awareness of God in life — is about as undenominational a concept as can be imagined. It largely replaces meditation which is apt to be narrowed to specific methods associated with a party outlook. The Tractarian allegiance of St. Ignatius Loyola stamped that movement with a kind of catholic party badge: this is here done away. Where meditation is retained it is broadened in such a way that it can only be placed under the good old ecumenical heading of Bible-reading.

The divine office, according to its 1662 Book of Common Prayer pattern, although adapted from a much wider tradition, is narrowly Anglican. This is replaced by the eucharistic-prologue-office which could easily take on an ecumenical significance. Jeremias is assuredly right in describing the Lord's Prayer as the original office in his signature tune or regimental march sense, for this prayer is the one absolutely common factor amongst all who call themselves Christians. Unlike the Bible or the historic creeds it is above and beyond divisive interpretation; it is our most obvious bond of unity. If, as a vast tradition dictates, there is value in slightly expanding the office, then the addition of psalmody and such classical hymns as *Te Deum* and *Gloria in Excelsis*, and of the familiar biblical canticles, could be of ecumenical value. For some time now Freechurchmen have become more and more appreciative of the value of some form of common prayer; what I have called the eucharistic-prologue-office might well overflow Anglican boundaries in a way that Mattins and Evensong will certainly not. Should any denominational difficulties arise from such a suggestion, the mutual working out of a very simple form of common prayer — which could be *really* common in a worldwide sense — might be a more worthy subject for dialogue than ecclesiastical and legalist schemes for superficial reunion. If we truly seek union, I suggest that common prayer might be a better start than common principle.

The centrality of the eucharist is unlikely to be a bone of contention among most of the churches, and the restricted stress on the calendar could be construed as a move towards a united centre. In my discussion on Christian community static parochialism — a peculiarity of the Church of England rather than of Anglicanism — was seen to be unlikely to meet the needs of our age.

In fine, this book is written from an Anglican viewpoint with no specifically ecumenical objective, yet in the course of what I hope is an objective study tight, old-fashioned Anglicanism takes something of a knock. If culture is a factor in theological formation this is not surprising; the ecumenical movement at this particular time is not the bright idea of a few Church leaders — not even of Pope John — but it has arisen as part of a cultural pattern.

These are infinite possibilities within the providential scheme of things; Christ reigns, and I have faith in the indwelling Spirit who spake by the prophets and continues so to speak: Glory be to Father, Son and Holy Ghost. Being-Being-Being: Holy-Holy-Holy.

INDEX

Index